RUNNING A
SUCCESSFUL
ADVERTISING
CAMPAIGN

The Daily Telegraph
ESSENTIAL MANAGEMENT TECHNIQUES

RUNNING A SUCCESSFUL ADVERTISING CAMPAIGN

IAIN MAITLAND

Published by Telegraph Publications,
Peterborough Court, At South Quay,
181 Marsh Wall, London E14 9SR

Series Editor: Marlene Garsia

Typeset by Bookworm Typesetting, Manchester
Printed in Great Britain by Biddles Ltd, Guildford

British Library Cataloguing in Publication Data
Maitland, Iain
    Running a successful advertising campaign.
    1. Advertising
    I. Title   II. Series
    659.1
ISBN 0–86367–288–4

Contents

Foreword

Every business must advertise to survive and prosper. That is a plain and simple fact. An advertising campaign may consist of advertisements on peak time television or a tiny caravan displaying goods in a local car park. They are both forms of advertising, without which business would be the poorer.

The most successful advertiser will carefully plan his campaign from start to finish. He will set his objectives and his budget and will research his market and the media. Ideas will be translated into potential advertisements and tried out. Then, and only then, will he proceed with his campaign, which will be evaluated at every stage. A cautious, careful approach is the key to success.

This book has been written for the manager who handles advertising in a larger company or the small businessman for whom an advertising agency fees may be prohibitively expensive. Advertising is a relatively simple, easy to understand subject which, unfortunately, has suffered at the hands of the professionals. This book cuts through the mystique and technical jargon, dealing with the important points of an advertising campaign in a clear and concise manner. You will find *Running a Successful Advertising Campaign* a useful reference source both now and in the future.

Iain Maitland
April 1988

1
Defining Advertising Objectives

A successful advertising campaign needs to be carefully planned right from the start. You must establish your objectives before setting an appropriate budget, research your market having precisely defined what or who constitutes the market at which your advertising is aimed, i.e. your target market, choose the media you intend to use and create interesting, well designed advertisements. Your objectives in advertising will vary and this fact will affect the type and style of campaign you choose.

Advertising objectives will usually fall into one of the following categories:

- To launch a new product.
- To remind.
- To reassure.
- To educate.
- To announce a change.
- To compete.
- To maintain sales.
- To please.
- To test.
- To recruit.
- To sell direct.

Let us now look at each of these objectives in more detail.

To Launch a New Product

Launching a new product or service into a fiercely competitive market place is a costly exercise. It is estimated that a budget equal to 25 per cent of the unit selling price may be required. Customers are notoriously slow to accept new ideas and are suspicious of innovations. For example, a new Vietnamese restaurant in a small provincial town would probably get off to a slow start because most of those people living in its catchment area would be reluctant to try something which falls outside their normal sphere of taste experience.

You will, therefore, need to have a campaign which is bright, bold and dramatic, implemented through a form of media which affords the most effective cover. A new shop, for instance, may advertise its presence on local radio, followed up with posters on billboards, notice boards and other suitable locations around the town, finally bringing people into the shop with an impressive window display. Advertisements must be repeated frequently to enhance market perception and persuade the public to buy a new product.

To Remind

Products and services need to be advertised regularly. This may not require a huge budget, but as customers' memories are short it is important to maintain good visibility. A continual campaign using window or car stickers, leaflet distribution, and display stands at the point of sale, will reinforce the message and keep your product in the customer's mind.

To Reassure

It is important to keep previous customers happy to ensure that they buy your product again. In addition, previous buyers of major items such as audio visual equipment, freezers or furniture, are invisible salesmen for your company. Their advice, based on product satisfaction, will influence potential customers far more than any advertisement or salesman can. A small budget could, perhaps, be allocated to keep previous buyers happy. An inexpensive, personalised direct mail campaign which seeks their opinion and gives them the latest news, will make the customer feel important, good about your company and will keep the product in their mind. Avoid advertisements which indicate a product is 'new' or 'improved'. They only make the previous buyers feel that they now have an inferior, second rate product, which creates bad feelings and may be counter-productive in the long term.

To Educate

Some products or services may require careful explanation as far as potential customers are concerned. In such cases your advertising objective will be not only to ensure that they are aware of a product but also of its full range of uses. For example, it is not enough for people to know of the existence of a financial consultant, they also need to know what he does, the services he offers and the benefits to themselves. Clearly, meeting these criteria will affect the advertiser's budget, choice of media and type of advertisement considerably. The financial consultant may, therefore, need to choose a medium, such as newspapers and magazines, where he has the space to fully explain his services.

To Announce a Change

Companies continually spend money on improving and updating their goods and it is important that you do not automatically assume that the customer will be aware of any change. Your advertising objective, therefore, will be to ensure that the customer knows that your product has altered in price, size or has been packaged differently. However, you must strike a careful balance between impressing potential new customers and not offending existing ones. Improvements are often greeted with annoyance by former purchasers, who are angry they have missed out. Alternatively an 'improvement' may be viewed with suspicion. Does the new, improved chocolate wrapper hide a smaller, less tasty bar? Through the use of sales promotion schemes and point of sale material, you must carefully try to please everyone – a difficult task.

To Compete

Often your objective may simply be to keep up with your competitors. For example, a direct competitor may have developed a new product to match that which your company already markets. When this happens, it is a natural instinct to advertise purely to challenge a competitor but you should be careful to avoid 'tit for tat' advertising, which will eat into your budget. Qualcast and Flymo, the lawnmower manufacturers, and the Electricity and Gas Boards have, in recent years, been drawn into such expensive battles which benefit no one. Often, money-off-coupons, vouchers, gifts or samples are sufficient to maintain market share for the retailer, whilst manufacturers can emphasize that they offer a proven product, at competitive prices, with good after sales service.

To Maintain Sales

However good your product or service is, it will not sell itself. In order to maintain sales, advertising must be a continual and regular process. Although the over all advertising objective will be to maintain sales, different campaigns with different budgets, target markets, media and advertisements, will be required at different times.

Products and services have varying life cycles. When the product or service is launched the campaign will require a large budget and full scale advertising in order to overcome consumer resistance. If successful, there may be a period of very rapid growth when little advertising may be required. Word of mouth often spreads demand, particularly with items which create a fashion or craze, e.g. Rubik's Cube and personal cassette players. A small budget will probably be sufficient to maintain or even increase sales using occasional advertising and good point of sale material.

At some stage the product reaches maturity, sales reach a plateau which can last for a few weeks or months and, in the case of some fashionable goods, for a lifetime. Products such as Bisto, Guinness and Hovis, for example, seem to sell continually year in year out. At this stage, advertising must really do its work to achieve the objective of maintaining sales. Your budget will need to be sufficient to remind and reassure, fight off competition and, more importantly, inform a volatile market.

Many advertisers fail to acknowledge that their customers can change almost daily. Previous purchasers move away, lose interest, stop using the goods or even die and new customers are continually coming into the market. A 'customer' is changing all the time, going from teenager to young married person, to parent and, eventually, to grandparent. They move regularly from one consumer group to another and goods which were previously of no interest become fascinating. A young man may have no interest in pensions and mortgages until he marries and, similarly, no interest in baby foods until he becomes a father. Regardless of any previous campaigns, you will need to advertise to attract new consumers as they join the target market. All previous advertising, however extensive, will have little relevance to the newcomer because they were not receptive at that time and are, therefore, unlikely to have absorbed the message.

Most products will, at some stage, enter a period of temporary or permanent decline. A temporary decline caused, for example, by competition or the time of year, will mean continual advertising is worthwhile. Indeed, you may decide to expand your advertising to attract new buyers. Say you produce a range of toiletries directed, through appropriate media, to the 15 to 24 age group, you may, by moving up into the 24 to 40 age group medium, attract new business. Alternatively, you may attempt to increase sales to current buyers by encouraging them to become heavy rather than light users. However, a natural, long term decline will rarely benefit from increased advertising. It may slow the slide down but, in truth, the money could be put to better use by developing new products or services which can, ultimately, replace those in decline.

To Please

Often, the objective may simply be to please. A small allocation for regular advertising through the right media to the right market will motivate your staff, sales force and customers. For the staff, it can be a morale booster as it makes them feel they work for a dynamic, go ahead company. It gives the sales force an opening line, a source of conversation and creates an impression of importance. Such advertising can be especially popular with stockists who may be operating on small margins and limited budgets. You may actually use their name, giving them the spin-off value from your advertisement. In return, they will be more inclined to order your goods and display them prominently, especially if attractive stands are supplied, because they know they have your support.

To Test

Another objective may be to test a medium, or a particular advertisement, to see how suitable it is for the product, how costly it is, what market it reaches and what responses it achieves. For example, you may want to compare the merits of the press and radio (see Chapter 4) or, because your market is specialised, try the use of direct mail, before deciding which approach is most suitable (refer to 'Creating an Advertisement'). It is vital that, in any campaign, you test the chosen medium carefully before committing your total budget. It pays to be cautious.

To Recruit

You may seek simply to recruit staff or, because you feel your product has insufficient outlets, may need to find additional distributors. In the case of staff recruitment, local advertising will often suffice, although it may be necessary to use trade journals or daily newspapers to attract senior managers and applicants with very specialised skills. This latter exercise can prove extremely expensive and you may decide it is more economical to use the services of a reputable employment agency instead. When looking for additional distributors, you may limit your budget and costs by direct appeals through the trade press. On the other hand, the decision could be to extend the budget and advertise to the consumer, perhaps also taking large advertisements to impress the trade. This tactic is used to increase consumer demand for the specific product leading, hopefully, to the point where the retailers will then approach you direct in order to stock such a popular item.

To Improve the Company's Image

Many advertisers choose to promote their company rather than individual products and for market leaders who produce a range of goods, this is often a wise method. Clearly, however, it can be difficult to assess the results.

To Sell Direct

Many businesses, for example, book or record clubs, sell direct to their customers through press advertisements, brochures or direct mail. The results of using such methods can easily be measured simply by counting the number of replies received. It is also a method which lends itself well to clearing out old stock and surplus goods.

As you can see, advertising objectives are many and varied and the list is potentially endless. However, the important point to keep in mind is that you establish your precise objectives before commencing a campaign. You cannot hit your target audience unless you know exactly where it is located.

2
Setting the Budget

Having decided your basic advertising objectives, your next step is to set a budget which will allow you to achieve those aims. The advertising appropriation, which is defined as 'the total sum of money to be spent on advertising over a fixed period' is, unfortunately, often seen as a luxury. Some companies believe that a good product or service will sell automatically and as a result advertising expenditure is unplanned.

Advertising plays an important role in any business. It is not the 'icing on the cake' but an essential ingredient. Every business must advertise, in one form or another, to succeed. A shopkeeper may proudly boast that he need never advertise but what about his window, that is his biggest advertisement. An accountant may not advertise his business in the normal way in the press, on television or radio but his name plate, stationery and insertion in *Yellow Pages* are all forms of advertising. Without the shopkeeper's window or the accountant's nameplate their businesses would be less visible to potential customers and would suffer accordingly.

An advertising appropriation should be carefully planned for odd amounts spent on an aimless campaign are wasted sums of money. Advertising expenditure should be part of the total marketing budget. It is, after all, part of the marketing process and is as important as distribution and selling. These facets must all be linked together to ensure that products and services are sold. Effective advertising will increase sales and, therefore, profit margins. It is a positive and primary cost which makes money and pays for itself several times over, hence its importance.

How much, however, should be spent? There are many theoretical text book solutions, ranging from a random figure based on the chairman's 'experience' to those derived from complex mathematical formulae. The most popular methods are worth consideration. Some will be of relevance, many will not and, after due thought and discussions, will be discarded. Whatever choice you make you will at least have viewed the situation from different angles, thought things through and made a plan.

Budgeting by Past Results

Many advertisers choose to base their future advertising budget or appropriation, on sales from previous years, employing one of the following methods.

Percentage of previous sales

Using this method, your appropriation will be based on a set percentage of the previous year's sales. It is linked to the idea that if £5,000 was spent last year to produce sales totalling £200,000, then an appropriation of £10,000 this year will lead to sales of £400,000.

Such a method, however, has drawbacks. It is difficult to decide on the percentage to use and often the decision will have to be a guess and, therefore, may be inaccurate. In addition, sales generally will fluctuate each year. The previous year's figures may have been good which, fortunately, would increase this year's advertising budget. Conversely, a bad previous year would lead to a smaller appropriation this year, when realistically you may require a larger budget to reverse the decline in sales or to launch a new product.

The idea that doubling last year's expenditure will double this year's sales figures is inaccurate. For example, two radio advertisements instead of one will not necessarily lead to two sets of sales. There are too many unconsidered contributory factors to take into account, e.g. when and at what time was the second advertisement broadcast? You may simply have reached the same audience twice or even appealed to the wrong market. Clearly, this method is of limited use on its own.

Historic method

An alternative method is to set a figure for the appropriation and allowing for increased costs, proportionally spend the same sum this year as last year and the year before. Again, there is the problem of settling on a rational figure. A sum set in 1987 is unlikely to be of relevance five or ten years later. Markets expand and contract, new products come and go, competition increases and decreases, media change and develop. Today television is a medium which is too costly for the smaller advertiser but the growth of cable and satellite television may, in five years time, change this. Your budget must be flexible to allow for such changes and this method is not.

Residual of previous surplus

This is a method adopted by many cautious businessmen who wish to balance the books. The idea of using excess money is, however, unscientific and illogical. It takes no account of current or future needs and, of course, a bad year would mean that there was little or no residue to use. This could take you into a downward spiral of no sales, no profit and no advertising eventually leading to less sales, losses and even total failure.

Budgeting for the Present

Having considered and learned from past experience (success or failure) you will then need to consider alternative methods of budgeting for advertising expenditure.

Gross margin method

Use of this method links appropriation to gross profit. The costs of producing and selling the goods are deducted from total sales and the appropriation is then fixed as a percentage of the remaining balance. There is, as always, the problem of fixing a suitable percentage. Very often, the manager using this method cannot truly understand the importance of advertising. It should be included in, and is as significant as, the costs of producing, distributing and selling and should not have to fight for the 'leftovers'. Any appropriation arrived at by this method will fluctuate conversely with profit. In other words, more money available in good years when it is not necessarily needed and in bad years, perhaps when a product is being relaunched, there will be little or no advertising budget at a time when the company needs it most.

Unit percentage method

In many ways, this method eliminates the guess work in setting a percentage as it links the appropriation to results. The cost of the goods is calculated so that each unit's costs are divided into a percentage for materials, production, advertising, transport, distribution and profit. The advertiser, planning to produce and sell a fixed number of units, can then calculate his advertising appropriation accordingly. This appears, in theory, to be an ideal method but you do need to be aware that internal costs and overheads are unlikely to remain constant and in proportion. The percentage must be regularly reviewed and, if necessary, revised. In addition, external factors will change; for example, media costs will rise and it may be expensive to constantly monitor an ever changing environment.

Comparative method

A popular method, much used by companies who have no previous records to refer to, is that of basing expenditure on that of their competitors. Larger advertisers can keep track of rival spending through such organisations as MEAL, Nielsens and Attwood (refer to page 39 'Research'). Even a small shopkeeper can, by checking his local press and listening to the radio, arrive at an approximation of what his competitors are spending. In theory, an increase in your appropriation above and beyond that of your rivals, will increase business accordingly.

You should bear in mind, however, that your research may be incomplete. You could be unaware that your rival distributes sales letters to his customers, hands leaflets out in the high street each week offering discounts and advertises in magazines that you do not read. Also, every business is different and products, services and markets all vary. The advertising expenditure for one business may be inappropriate to another; for example, your rival shopkeeper may have a prime high street position between Marks & Spencer's and W H Smith's, therefore he will need to spend far less on advertising than a shop on the outskirts of town.

Arbitrary method

Many advertisers, particularly smaller ones, budget in an arbitrary way. They do not calculate an appropriation for the forthcoming year on a percentage or proportional basis of past or future figures, but will spend whatever they can afford at the time. With this method, the advertiser will often spend as and when required. Perhaps he hears of a new competitor or a pretty salesgirl catches him on a good day. Alternatively, he may occasionally like to see his name in print as it may make him feel good or look important. It is a method which has no logic, no plan, no thought and absolutely no chance of success.

Budgeting on Future Performance

In many ways, looking to the future to calculate a budget is more sensible than looking to the past. After all, such a budget must operate in the future, not in the past. However, as you will see in the following sections, there are certain drawbacks.

Percentage of future sales

A much more progressive and realistic approach than basing a budget on past sales. However, it again invites an arbitrary and inaccurate choice of a percentage. It is also difficult to predict the future. There are too many unknown factors which could lead to over or to under spending.

Residual of anticipated surplus

Similarly, this method invites problems with forecasting the future. Products may decrease in popularity, for example, and costs may rise. The use of a residue has the same drawbacks as preparing a budget based on residue of past sales.

Target methods

Such methods are increasingly popular and rightly so because they acknowledge the primary importance of advertising. The advertiser sets an objective, which may be a target of selling a particular quantity of goods, of reaching a particular number of people or even establishing a new product in a particular region. Based on this target you must then calculate how much it will cost to achieve your target and the best way of doing so.

For example, you may seek to advertise to a certain number of young mothers. By researching your media (see page 34), you discover that there are five national 'baby' magazines who reach your target market. You can then compare and calculate costs. Do, however, bear in mind that there are other factors to be taken into consideration in making the choice. Should you choose a weekly or monthly magazine, a page or half page advertisement, colour or black and white? Chapter 4 on the media will help you to resolve these problems.

Clearly, all these methods of setting a budget have individual benefits and drawbacks. None are wholly right or wrong and which you choose depends to a great degree on the specific business you are in. For example, the owner of a seaside guest house may have a number of rooms to let during the summer months, when her regular clientele of students from the nearby polytechnic have gone home for the holidays. From past experience, she knows that if she spends a set sum each year advertising in the local tourist office, all her rooms will be let. An increased budget will not increase profit because she only has a limited number of rooms and any decrease would probably result in rooms staying empty. In this instance the historic method of budgeting is ideal for her.

Alternatively, the businessman who has just started to

manufacture a revolutionary new product has no historic basis on which to work and no competition with which to compare. Therefore, the target methods will be the most suitable for him to use.

In common with the majority of advertisers you will, in fact, usually budget on a composite basis, mixing two or more of the methods previously outlined. You will look and learn from the past few years, compare the sales figures with previous appropriations, seasons and trends; consider your current situation, taking into account the range and costs of available media, current market conditions, competition and, finally, look to the future. Have past appropriations produced satisfactory results? In the light of expected costs, sales and profits, is this amount still satisfactory for the forthcoming year?

There is, unfortunately, no simple answer. You cannot, by any method, calculate precisely that a certain sum or percentage is required for no one actually knows. All that you can do is attempt to view the overall situation from every angle taking into consideration as many influencing factors as you are aware of. Set a flexible budget which allows for change, for example, increased advertising or the use of a different media, if required. You may, for instance, choose to set a minimum and maximum limit within which to work.

It is almost impossible to know if an increased budget would have increased sales or not and, conversely, whether the same results could have been achieved with less advertising. Only experience mixed with good sense, flair, imagination and a degree of luck will bring the best results.

3
Research

Having established precise advertising objectives and settled on a flexible and sufficient budget, you must then initiate a policy of continuous research and assessment. Market research may be defined as a study of existing or potential goods and services and their markets. Research is vital before, during and after an advertising campaign. It can help you to define a target audience, choose the correct medium and create the right advertisement. During a campaign, it can be used as a check to ensure everything is running smoothly and effectively. Once the campaign is over, continued research can measure its success. Market research can normally be divided into two categories, desk research and field research.

Desk Research

It is essential that you continually study available published material in order to obtain up-to-date information on an ever changing situation. There is a wealth of literature available from a wide range of sources. A study of your own company's internal records would, for example, indicate previous advertisements used, their costs, choice of media and the success of the campaign. Trade, professional and technical associations often produce reports and surveys on, for instance, 'the consumer' and these are published in trade papers or magazines. Media owners and specialist organisations (see page 34 'Researching the Media') produce information on types of readers, circulations and advertising rates. The government produce statistics which will indicate changes in, say, the economic environment, indicating that people being employed in a certain region receive higher salaries, have more television, videos and so on. You need to be aware of all the changes that occur around you, which may affect the size and type of campaign you plan.

Field Research

Alternatively you can, perhaps by employing a specialist agency, compile your own statistics by interviewing customers 'in the field'. Such research may be on a 'one off' basis, perhaps to judge if there is a market for a new product, or a continuous basis, for example, to see how a product is progressing in popularity. For such research to be meaningful, you will need to establish a 'sample', which essentially is a mixed group of people large enough to represent the total target market. The sample group should have the same perceived characteristics as the whole, in order to obtain an accurate response. You may decide to select a 'quota sample' whereby the interviewer will seek out people who fulfil the basic characteristics of sex, age and so on. Instead, you may select a 'random sample', where the interviewer approaches specific names at particular addresses based, say, on the ACORN system (refer to page 31 'Researching the Market'). Surveys can be conducted on the telephone, by post, by stopping people on the street or on a panel basis. This last method can involve groups of people completing a diary indicating actions or purchases over a period of time.

It does not fall within the scope of this book to detail the practicalities of market research. Other books are available which document the subject more fully and a selection of these is detailed in the Bibliography on page 133. However, you do need to be aware of the necessity for thorough researching and keeping up-to-date with your business, its products, policies, competition, market and the media. A carefully planned campaign has a greater chance of success than one based on hunches or 'feelings'.

Researching the Organisation

Initially, it is important for any advertiser to study his business and those products or services which will affect the type of advertising campaign introduced.

First, you should consider the company's current public image. Is it good, bad or, perhaps, unknown? If it is highly regarded and known, you may decide to adopt a 'reminder' rather than an 'informative' approach. Market leaders, such as Silver Cross in the baby market, might advertise its name with the phrase 'simply the best', which is short and easy to remember. A new company in the same trade will need more time, more space and more frequent advertising to supply detailed information and it may still be less effective. Similarly, a company with a 'bad' image may need to spend more to change the consumer's perception. Do not forget to also consider whether your business is viewed as well established, solid, respectable and full of tradition – qualities to be promoted – or whether it is seen as dull and old fashioned – an image which needs updating. Similarly, the company may be viewed as dynamic and forward looking or brash and over confident. Clearly, in such a case you will need to decide whether you wish to promote or, perhaps, change that image.

Second, you need to consider whether the business has any limitations. Is it well sited? A wholesale business, for example, may boast a nationwide service and van delivery. However, if it was sited in Land's End it would hardly wish to promote its 'free van delivery' in John O'Groats. Can it produce enough goods or services? The home based mother and daughter business which makes handmade sweaters would be ill advised to advertise nationally because they would, in all probability, be unable to cope with the demand. Can the company offer a good after sales service? Many customers buy particular goods if they are convinced that faults will be quickly and smoothly repaired. The established company with an efficient service department might decide to advertise guarantees and 'repair promises', also informing retailers through trade papers. If, however, the company was new, offered imported goods and was not yet in a position to offer such a service, it would need to look for another angle to promote in its advertising.

Third, bear in mind the past and present policies of your

business. As indicated, launching a new product will require a different campaign with large, informative, widespread advertising, whilst the product which has reached maturity only needs the occasional reminder advertisement, perhaps at point of sale, to nudge the customer into a purchase. Your company may be seeking to increase sales in a particular region by using selected regional media. If you are looking for increased sales frequency amongst existing purchasers, the use of 'money off next purchase' vouchers or a free gift in return for so many packet tops offer could be the answer. You may be looking to attract totally new customers by, for instance, advertising in a different medium and targeting the advertising towards a different age group. A range of lingerie selling well to the 15 to 24 age group and advertised through magazines such as *Just Seventeen* and *Nineteen*, might run a campaign in *Woman's Own* or *Woman* adapted to promote a more mature image.

Fourth, the product or service is equally important. You should consider the price. If it is cheap and offers good value for money, then that may be the most important factor which should be promoted. Such goods are likely to have a more general appeal and be advertised through the tabloid papers rather than the 'quality' press. Alternatively, if the product is expensive then the choice of media used would probably be reversed and product quality would be promoted in preference to price.

Fifth, you must also consider the product's other attributes. You may promote its size; for example, Andrex toilet tissue claims to be bigger, longer and stronger than its competitors.

Colour may be your choice – 'The widest choice of paints in town'. Or what about packaging? An unusual or distinctive packet could form the central point of the advertisement. Benson and Hedges, for example, use their 'gold' cigarette packets within their advertisement to great effect. Your product may also have several uses. The versatility of the food processer which blends, mixes and chops or the pram which converts into a carrycot and pushchair, are all points to be stressed.

Finally, before researching the market, you should consider your competition on the same basis as you study your own business. Highlight their individual strengths and weaknesses and perhaps plan a campaign around this. If, for instance, they are perceived as being expensive then you may possibly choose to promote the price of your product.

Researching the Market

It is vital to be aware of your precise target market in order that your campaign can be directed to the right audience, through the right medium, at the right time and in the right way. To succeed, you must have a clear picture and comprehensive understanding of your potential customers.

You must, firstly, consider the demographic difference between customers and non-customers. Are you aiming your advertising at a particular sex? The suppliers of perfume, cosmetics and stockings are looking at an audience of women and this would clearly affect the choice of media – women's magazines rather than general interest magazines. It could also affect the timing, as surveys show that housewives listen to the radio in the morning rather than the afternoon or evening; and the style of the campaign, allowing for a soft, gentle and informative approach rather than a hard hitting one. Look next at the age and status of the audience. Many companies divide the market into age groups of 15 to 24 years, 24 to 35 years and so on. In addition, you will need to consider whether the consumer is single, engaged, married, divorced or widowed. A pensions fund company, for example, will generally expect to attract a mix of men and women, but then needs to consider that the majority of those in the age range 15–24 years will probably not yet be interested in the product because they are single and have no ties. In this case the pension fund company would, initially, seek to attract those in the 24–35 age range who are engaged, married or young parents. With this general group in mind, advertising can be targeted through the appropriate medium. For example, the cinema which mainly attracts the 15 to 24 age range could be eliminated but the press most read by your target market or direct mail actively considered. From this, the correct time and type of advertisement could be chosen.

They may, for example, advertise in a Sunday paper where they have time to explain the benefits in a medium which is likely to be read in a leisurely and relaxed atmosphere.

The advertising campaign may also be influenced by the average income of the market. A pension fund or life assurance scheme advertising campaign would have little success if it was sent by direct mail to those on the lowest levels of income. What the advertiser is looking for are those people with sufficient income to allow them to make the necessary investment.

Many advertisers will view customers in a mixture of ways, taking into account sex, age, status, income and their 'social grade', i.e. are they upper, middle or working class? The National Readership Surveys, conducted by JICNARS, bases its six social grades upon the occupation, not the income, of the head of the household. These social grades are:

- A – Upper middle class. Executive, senior managerial, administrative or professional position. Of the population, 3 per cent are designated as 'A' grades.
- B – Middle class. Middle management, administrative or professional position; 13 per cent of the population are 'B' grades.
- C1 – Lower middle class. Junior management, administrative or professional position. Alternatively, a tradesman or other non-manual worker. Of the population 22 per cent are 'C1' grades.
- C2 – Skilled working class. Skilled manual worker who has normally served an apprenticeship; 32 per cent of the population are 'C2' grades.
- D – Working class. Semi- or un-skilled manual worker; 19 per cent of the population are 'D' grades.
- E – Lowest subsistence levels. Pensioner, widow, casual worker or the unemployed; 11 per cent of the population are 'E' grades.

A financial consultant would, therefore, aim his advertising to mainly A and B grades through 'AB' media – *The Daily* or *Sunday Telegraph* rather than *The Sun*, a business management exhibition rather than a general interest one.

You will also need to know where the audience is. Are they local, in a particular region, scattered across the country, Europe or even the world? Clearly, local radio, cinema or press advertising may be inappropriate to a scattered special interest group. In this case, an advertiser might prefer to use a trade or hobby magazine or, alternatively, direct mail to specific, named individuals. The market might consist of half-a-dozen other businesses rather than individuals, in which case the same media may be used but a different approach adopted because a business may perceive a purchase in a different way to the individual.

Having established the demographic make up of an audience, you may wish to consider the potential customer's lifestyle, his interests, attitudes and activities which can cut across all demographic factors. Clearly, an interest in football, rugby or skiing equipment need not be restricted to a particular class or income level. A popular method of viewing the market in this way is based on ACORN (A Classification of Residential Neighbourhoods). Compiled on census statistics, this system considers a range of variables, from demography through to employment, and divides the population into different neighbourhood types within different groups. The ACORN system is based on postal geography and postcodes. It is the ideal basis for some direct mail campaigns because each individual address will indicate the occupant's probable lifestyle.

Table 3.1 *ACORN classifications*

Acorn groups		1985 population	%
A	Agricultural areas	1837585	3.4
B	Modern family housing, higher incomes	9056851	16.8
C	Older housing of intermediate status	9519639	17.7
D	Older terraced housing	2309097	4.3
E	Council estates – category I	7015875	13.0
F	Council estates – category II	4892746	9.1
G	Council estates – category III	3935124	7.3
H	Mixed inner metropolitan areas	2088892	3.9
I	High status non-family areas	2265371	4.2
J	Affluent suburban housing	8531179	15.9
K	Better-off retirement areas	2048658	3.8

Acorn types

A	1	Agricultural villages	1404704	2.6
A	2	Areas of farms and smallholdings	432881	0.8
B	3	Post-war functional private housing	2276963	4.2
B	4	Modern private housing, young families	1805955	3.4
B	5	Established private family housing	3173195	5.9
B	6	New detached houses, young families	1475680	2.7
B	7	Military bases	325058	0.6
C	8	Mixed owner-occupied and council estates	1877008	3.5
C	9	Small town centres and flats above shops	2185911	4.1
C	10	Villages with non-farm employment	2523830	4.7
C	11	Older private housing, skilled workers	2932890	5.5
D	12	Unmodernised terraces, older people	1349349	2.5
D	13	Older terraces, lower income families	752530	1.4
D	14	Tenement flats lacking amenities	207218	0.4
E	15	Council estates, well-off older workers	1879887	3.5
E	16	Recent council estates	1460237	2.7
E	17	Better council estates, younger workers	2642427	4.9
E	18	Small council houses, often Scottish	1033324	1.9
F	19	Low rise estates in industrial towns	2498587	4.6
F	20	Inter-war council estates, older people	1607711	3.0
F	21	Council housing, elderly people	786448	1.5
G	22	New council estates in inner cities	1075117	2.0
G	23	Overspill estates, higher unemployment	1678631	3.1
G	24	Council estates with some overcrowding	839998	1.6
G	25	Council estates with greatest hardship	341378	0.6
H	26	Multi-occupied older housing	204279	0.4
H	27	Cosmopolitan owner-occupied terraces	577592	1.1
H	28	Multi-let housing in cosmopolitan areas	388292	0.7
H	29	Better-off cosmopolitan areas	918729	1.7
I	30	High status non-family areas	1132770	2.1
I	31	Multi-let big old houses and flats	833500	1.5
I	32	Furnished flats, mostly single people	299101	0.6
J	33	Inter-war semis, white collar workers	3056752	5.7
J	34	Spacious inter-war semis, big gardens	2671266	5.0
J	35	Villages with wealthy older commuters	1560179	2.9
J	36	Detached houses, exclusive suburbs	1242982	2.3
K	37	Private houses, well-off older residents	1204778	2.2
K	38	Private flats, older single people	843880	1.6
U	39	Unclassified	294080	0.5
Area Total			53795097	100.0

Reproduced by permission of Acorn

Researching the Media

The media, their characteristics, benefits and drawbacks are discussed in Chapter 4. However, there are a number of organisations who you can approach to obtain the information and statistical analyses needed to refer to before making your final decision. The following list gives their names, addresses and telephone numbers, together with a brief synopsis of the facilities they provide.

The Advertising Association
15 Wilton Road
London SW1V 1NJ
01–828 2771

AA represents the widest range of advertisers, media, agencies and associated services. It is an excellent source of information, publishing reports and statistics on advertising, including the *International Journal of Advertising* and the *Quarterly Forecast of Advertising Expenditure*.

The Advertising Standards Authority
2–16 Torrington Place
London WC1E 7HN
01–580 5555
ASA investigates complaints concerning advertisements which might contravene the British Code of Advertising Practice. A free advisory and pre-publication service is available. Informative case reports are also regularly published.

Association of Free Newspapers
Ladybellegate House
Longsmith Street
Gloucester GL1 2HT
0452 308100
The Association has a trade membership of free newspaper titles and can assist with research into free papers.

Association of Independent Radio Contractors
259–269 Marylebone Road
London NW1 5RA
01–262 6681

AIRC is the trade association for the independent radio companies.

Audit Bureau of Circulations
13 Wimpole Street
London W1M 7AB
01–631 1343
ABC is a tripartite-based company consisting of advertisers, advertising agencies and publishers. Its role is to check and certify publishers' audited circulation figures. Circulation, which may be defined as the number of copies actually purchased, compared to readership which could be far higher, is strictly based on net sales and excludes returned, unsold, undelivered or free copies. The audited figure of sales per day, week or month is issued on a six monthly basis. Controlled circulation and free distribution papers, through 'verified free distributions', can also be audited. ABC also audits, in terms of quality and quantity, visitors to exhibitions.

British Direct Marketing Association
1 New Oxford Street
London WC1A 1NQ
01–242 2254
BDMA represents the mail order industry and seeks to promote its image and reputation. It supplies informative guidelines, publications and bulletins including *BDMA News*.

British Exhibition Contractors Association
Kingsmere House
Graham Road
London SW19 3SR
01–543 3888
BECA members are involved with all aspects of exhibitions and are required to adhere to a strict code of conduct.

British Rate and Data
76 Oxford Street
London W1N 0HN
01–434 2233
BRAD is published each month by Maclean-Hunter Limited of 30 Old Burlington Street, London W1X 2AE. It supplies

information on the press, television, radio, posters, cinema and exhibition advertising. It details current ABC circulation figures, rates, requirements and current staff. In addition, BRAD publishes directories, annuals and advertiser/agency lists. It is probably the best buy for any serious advertiser.

Broadcasting Audience Research Board
52–56 Mortimer Street
London W1N 8AN
01–636 6866
BARB is an organisation set up by the BBC and ITCA to monitor television audiences. To measure the watching audience, a number of electronic meters are attached to television sets in a sample of homes. The meter records when the television is on and which station is being watched. BARB subsequently issues reports of detailed audience analysis. To judge audience reaction to programmes, BARB conducts around a thousand interviews each day.

Cinema Advertising Association
127 Wardour Street
London W1V 4AD
01–439 9531
CAA is the trade association for the UK's cinema advertising contractors. Also to maintain advertising standards throughout the industry, it supplies data on cinema admissions, audiences and campaigns.

Direct Mail Sales Bureau
12–13 Henrietta Street
London WC2E 8JJ
01–379 7531
DMSB is run by the direct mail industry and the Post Office. It provides help in the planning, creation, execution and evaluation of direct mail campaigns and publishes the *Planners Guide to Direct Mail.*

Incorporated Society of British Advertisers Limited
44 Hertford Street
London W1Y 8AE
01–499 7502
ISBA represents advertisers and publishes newsletters, reports and guides on all aspects of advertising.

Independent Television Companies Association
56 Mortimer Street
London W1N 8AN
01–636 6866
ITCA is the trade association of the programme companies and supplies details of television coverage, viewing and costs.

Institute of Practitioners in Advertising
44 Belgrave Square
London SW1X 8QS
01–235 7020
IPA represents advertising agencies, many of which charge fees affordable only by the very largest companies. However, they do still supply useful statistical data which is well worth reading.

Joint Industry Committee for National Readership Surveys
44 Belgrave Square
London SW1 8QS
01–235 7020
JICNARS represents the Press Council, the Institute of Practitioners in Advertising and the Incorporated Society of British Advertisers. Every year they conduct 30,000 interviews, based on social grades and designed to analyse who reads what. The questionnaire also includes questions on television, radio and cinema habits.

Joint Industry Committee for Poster Audience Research
3 Dean Farrar Street
London SW1H 9LG
01–222 0441
JICPAR represents the Outdoor Advertising Association of

Great Britain, the Incorporated Society of British Advertisers, the Institute of Practitioners in Advertising and the Council of Outdoor Specialists. The committee has data available on poster sites, and their potential audiences, throughout the country.

Joint Industry Committee for Radio Audience Research
44 Belgrave Square
London SW1X 8QS
01-235 7020
JICRAR represents the Institute of Practitioners in Advertising, the Incorporated Society of British Advertisers and the Association of Independent Radio Contractors. The local radio stations around the country who are members of AIRC regularly research their audiences and JICRAR subsequently publish reports of audience ratings, on a half hourly basis for the week. These supply details of listeners' age, sex and social grades.

Media Audits Limited
16 Dufours Place
London W1V 1FE
01-734 4080
MAL provides a consultancy service on advertising media.

Media Expenditure Analysis Limited
142 The Strand
London WC2R 1HH
01-240 1903
MEAL provides information on advertising expenditure of specific products, in order that the advertiser can gauge the extent of advertising within his market. It is an ideal source for discovering what rival firms are spending.

Outdoor Advertising Association
3 Dean Farrar Street
London SW1H 9LG
01-222 7988
The association is the trade organisation of poster contractors linked to JICPAR and PAB.

Poster Audit Bureau
Tower House
Southampton Street
London WC2E 7HN
01–836 1511
PAB represents the ISBA, IPA and poster contractors and its main role is to check that the right poster was in the right place at the right time and in good condition. It maintains a master file of poster sites and is a source of information and advice.

Radio Marketing Bureau
259–269 Old Marylebone Road
London NW1 5RA
01–258 3705
RMB is a source of marketing information for advertisers. It supplies booklets on radio advertising on ILR stations and its effect.

Regional Newspaper Advertising Bureau
141–143 Drury Lane
London WC2B 5TD
01–836 8251
RNAB represents regional newspapers and its aim is to supply information and services to advertisers who are considering the regional press as an advertising medium. It offers a central booking service, leaflets, and maintains full details on regional press research.

Target Group Index
53 The Mall
London W5 3TE
01–579 0417
A survey on products and media available on subscription. It indicates who buys what, in what quantities, why they like the products and which media are most suitable for advertising purposes.

Verified Free Distribution Limited
13 Wimpole Street
London W1M 7AB
01–631 1343
VFD is a subsidiary of ABC and certifies the circulation of the free distribution press.

4
Above the Line

A medium is the vehicle through which an advertiser reaches his audience. In order for an advertising campaign to succeed, the advertiser must choose the right medium, or media, for his product or service and advertise at the right time and to the right audience. Media are often divided into two categories:

- Above the line.
- Below the line.

Above the line is a purely artificial term carried by advertising agencies, which refers to the popular and traditional media:

- The press.
- Television.
- Radio.
- Outdoor (posters).
- Cinema.

Below the line refers to the less visible media:

- Direct mail.
- Exhibitions.
- Sales promotion.
- Point of sale material.
- Sales literature.

Below the line media is sometimes dismissed as unimportant, but the successful advertiser normally uses a mix of media. Each medium has a role to play and its own individual benefits and drawbacks, as will be seen in the following chapters.

The Press

In the UK the press is the most popular advertising medium. It accounts for 40 per cent of all advertising expenditure – an impressive percentage considering the range of media available.

Characteristics

The press is amazingly diverse. The advertiser can choose to advertise in newspapers or magazines. He can advertise nationally in daily or Sunday newspapers, such as *The Sunday Telegraph* or *The Sunday Times,* regionally in the dailies, bi-weeklies or local Sunday newspapers such as Plymouth's *Independent,* Birmingham's *Sunday Mercury* or Newcastle's *Sunday Sun.* In addition, there are in most towns and cities a host of free sheets.

Magazines are even more versatile. Here advertisers can choose between 'special interest' magazines as diverse as *Country Life, Punch* and *Penthouse,* through trade magazines such as *The Grocer* and *Cycle Trader,* to technical and professional magazines aimed at teachers, doctors, plumbers and so on. He can also consider a multitude of house magazines, directories, yearbooks, timetables and reference books which also carry advertisements.

The market

The range and depth of publications available is phenomenal. There are, for example, over 700 local free sheets and 3,000 trade and technical magazines in the UK.

With such a selection, you can target a specific audience tailor-made for your particular business. You will also be aware from the preceeding text on media research, that there is a wealth of audience information available from such sources as BRAD and JICNARS to aid you further in choosing the perfect outlets within each medium. For example, national newspapers offer mass circulation and high coverage, ideal for the advertiser of popular consumer goods. Each newspaper has its own style and appeals to different readership groups. *The Daily Telegraph* and *The Times*, for instance, have an ABC1 readership in the region of 80 and 85 per cent, whereas newspapers such as *The Sun* and *The Daily Mirror* only have around 20 to 25 per cent. Advertisers of upmarket products or services can choose one paper, whilst the advertiser of goods with popular appeal can choose another. AB businesses would select a newspaper such as *The Times, The Daily Telegraph* or *The Independent* in which to advertise. The owner of a loan finance company would probably have more success advertising in the tabloid press.

Local free sheets in recent years have increased in popularity to the stage where because of distribution methods they are received today by 90 per cent of the population. Of those householders, some 25 per cent buy goods or services advertised within these free sheets.

Clearly, the readership will vary according to each region. A loan finance company might choose to advertise in the high unemployment areas where there is likely to be more need for their services. However, since the introduction of the Finance Services Act any company offering investment or banking advice must follow the Securities Investment Board's rulings and those of the five regulatory organisations, as well as being a member of one. Other Acts have also to be observed when advertising goods, ranging from the Consumer Credit Act to the ruling on Health and Safety Warnings on, say, cigarette packets.

Consider also the many national, general interest magazines such as *Woman's Own, Woman, Homes & Gardens.* Ideal media if your target market is the housewife. For most audiences there are bound to be matching magazines. How many people have heard of *Cleaning and Maintenance, Heating and Ventilating Engineer* or *Brushes and Brushmaking International?*

Advantages

The press offers the advertiser the following benefits.

• **Flexibility**
As already outlined, the press offers such variety and scope that

you can easily appeal to specific groups on a national, local or 'interest' basis. You can reach both sexes, all ages, all income levels and all interests. In national newspapers you can have different copy in different editions – advertising umbrellas in Manchester and parasols in Torquay. Advertisements can be inserted and copy changed at very short notice. Often it is possible to use colour, illustrations or diagrams to enhance the message or you can simply rely on text. Advertisements can be booked to appear on a given day, in a given area and in a specific place within the newspaper or magazine. The television retailer can advertise opposite the 'What's On Page', the perfumery company opposite the women's page.

● The written word
An advertisement in the press should contain precise and detailed information. You have the time and space to tell a story or paint a picture for the reader. Your message can be read, re-read, filed away for future reference and kept for years. It is an intransient, permanent medium.

● Low cost
It is a relatively cheap and efficient way of reaching either a large number of scattered and unidentified potential customers or a small number of identified ones.

● Measurable response
It is a medium where you can easily judge success by the use of coupons, freepost, cards or coded replies. Therefore, it is ideal for mail order businesses, record or book clubs, holiday companies, travel agents or pools promoters.

Disadvantages
The press, however, has several drawbacks as an advertising medium.

● The unseen advertisement
The majority of the population and, therefore, your target

audience, do not read newspapers or magazines. The percentage of trade and professional people who read even their own industry's specialised magazines is often a relatively small proportion of the total potential market. To a degree your advertisement budget is wasted. In addition those who read the newspapers or magazines you advertise in do so selectively. The reader of a national newspaper may look at the city, sports or television pages or do the crossword but will rarely read it all from cover to cover, except perhaps on a Saturday or Sunday when there is more leisure time. Even the reader of a special magazine will read selectively. A housewife may read the letters or problem pages but flick through the romance story or knitting section without a glance. In other words, very few people read and absorb the printed word – including your advertisement – in relation to the number of copies which are sold.

- **Short life**

Most newspapers are quickly disposed of. The daily newspapers will last for no more than one day. Often it will be thrown away even sooner as it may have been purchased to occupy time on a train journey to work, to read over lunch, or to check city prices or football scores. Few papers purchased on the way to work reach home in the evening. Many housewives will not see them. However, weekly or monthly magazines may be kept longer or passed around among friends or relatives and may be more suitable for advertising purposes, depending on your goods and services.

- **Poor quality**

The majority of newspapers and many magazines are badly printed on poor quality paper. Advertisements that appear impressive when designed may be less effective through poor reproduction, smudging of the ink or text printed on one page showing through on the following one. It is not unknown for money-off vouchers or coupons to be printed back to back.

- **Static**

The press as an advertising medium lacks sound, movement,

realism, and the ability to demonstrate. It must overcome these drawbacks with good creative copy, which can be difficult to achieve (refer to 'Creating an Advertisement'). A 'run of the mill' advertisement is uninteresting and easy to miss.

These advantages and disadvantages must be taken into account when making your decision to use newspapers and magazines as part of your overall advertising campaign.

Television

As an advertising medium, television is prohibitively expensive for most companies and at the present time is, therefore, rarely used by the smaller advertiser. However, with the anticipated growth of satellite and cable television, it is a medium which could become much more accessible. With this in mind it has been included.

Characteristics

There are 15 programme contractors in the UK from London Weekend Television and Thames Television in London, reaching 19.6 per cent of homes, through to Channel Television in the Channel Islands reaching just 0.2 per cent. Across the country, it is a regional medium which reaches virtually the entire population. Some 98 per cent of homes have a television and a third of homes have more than one set. It is the country's leading leisure activity. In an average week, 86 per cent of all adults tune into Independent Television, with the average viewer watching it for over three hours each day. As an advertising medium, it offers sound, vision, movement, colour and a widespread mass audience.

The market

The television audience is perhaps the most thoroughly researched. It is an established fact that C2DE classes are generally 'heavy viewers' as opposed to ABs who are classified as 'light'.

Similarly, young adults with wider leisure interests will watch television far less than older, married couples such as pensioners with time on their hands. It is, however, also clear that different programmes will attract different types. Given an audience ranging from 500,000 to 20 million, it is best suited to mass appeal consumer goods, although there is room for choice. For instance, the advertiser of sports equipment would choose to advertise to young men around the Sunday afternoon football match, while the advertiser selling household cleaning items would undoubtedly select to buy time around *Coronation Street* or *Neighbours*.

Advantages

Television has a number of benefits.

• Complete

As indicated, television is in many ways a complete medium. It offers a picture, movement, the ability to demonstrate, colour and sound in addition to a high standard of presentation and a large attentive audience. Very little effort or concentration is required to absorb the advertising message, although the attention span of the average viewer does vary.

• Flexible

The advertiser can advertise where he likes, perhaps launching and testing a product in a particular region. He can target an advert around a particular programme and can repeat it as often as he likes – even in the same segment. Hamlet Cigars, for example, were very successful with a double advertisement in the same segment, the first part leaving the viewer with the feeling of 'what happens next?'. Today, advertising space is available for twenty-four hours each day in some regions. The growth of breakfast television, all night television and Channel Four has opened the advertising door to smaller businesses who can limit their advertisements to off peak, lightly viewed segments. In the early days of Channel Four many smaller businesses were able to take advantage of the preferential advertising rates being offered and some achieved a measure of success in this way.

● **Reliable data**
There is a wealth of research on television available which allows advertisers to select the right time for their products.

Disadvantages

For the smaller advertiser in particular, the drawbacks of television far outweigh the benefits.

● **Cost**
Airtime and production costs are colossal. The medium is largely limited to international and major national companies advertising mass market goods. Local advertisers are often limited to group advertising, perhaps for a particular town or shopping centre.

● **Waste**
Blanket, mass coverage is of little use to the advertiser who seeks to appeal to a limited audience or area. Too many people will see the advertisement who will not be interested in the product or service offered.

● **Transient**
The television is a very fleeting medium with a constant stream of instantly forgettable advertisements. It is only the very large companies who can afford continuous television advertising, whose advertising slogans tend to be remembered by viewers.

● **Enquiries**
Television is a difficult medium for attracting enquiries because the advertisement has gone within seconds. Longer advertisements are tedious and constant repeats can be irritating, unless the content is of a very high standard.

Radio

Radio is available for advertising on a local and national basis through the Independent Local Radio Network. By the 1990s, this network will incorporate approximately 70 regional stations reaching in total around 95 per cent of the population. Local radio is often more popular, in its region, than national radio.

Characteristics

Commercial radio offers a blend of popular music, talk shows, phone-ins and local, national and international news. It is a source of information, entertainment and companionship. The radio is usually switched on when other tasks, such as washing, cooking or driving are being carried out. It is rarely, except at news peaks, listened to exclusively but is often a semi-permanent 'background noise'. Advertisements, relying on sound only to convey the message, need to be brief, catchy and memorable – maximum use must be made of each word (refer to 'Creating an Advertisement').

The market

It is estimated that a third of the population listen to local radio each week and the majority are permanently tuned in to one station, which they listen to at the same time every day. The housewife who listens to London's Capital Radio on a Monday morning will also tune in on Tuesday, Wednesday, Thursday and Friday. It is a habit.

Radio is turned on mainly outside peak television hours and is most popular between 6.00 am and 9.00 am during the week. It is a medium which is particularly popular with young people interested in 'pop' music, which is the backbone of most radio stations. A Radio Luxembourg survey in the early 1980s indicated that in a one week period an average of 27 per cent of the audience were in the 13–18 year old age bracket.

The radio audience can be divided into general listening groups, according to the time of day. As a broad generalisation, the main audience between 6.00 am and 9.00 am are families at breakfast preparing to leave home or car drivers travelling to work. Between 9.00 am and 4.00 pm, a large majority of listeners are housewives, the unemployed, senior citizens and, during holidays, school children and students. After 4.00 pm and into the evening, young adults and car drivers on the way home tune in regularly. In the early hours, the audience consist largely of shift workers and insomniacs. At the weekend, especially on Sunday mornings, the audience is at leisure and comprises a cross section of the population, once again dominated by the younger age groups. Advertisements may be longer, more detailed and aimed at those looking for something to do or somewhere to go.

Advantages

Local radio can offer the advertiser the benefits of:

- **Sound**

The human voice is an immensely powerful selling aid if used well. It can convey a full range of emotions, from drama through to humour. In addition, music can be used to attract attention and create moods or feelings. Background noises can create or enhance a situation. A good radio advertisement can draw the listener into a world of his own.

- **Personality**

Radio is a very personable medium with its own individual 'feel', local personalities and roots with local charities and events. It is often friendly, approachable, sensitive, cosy and intimate. It is part of the local community, providing help and information during bad weather, publicity for local organisations and entertainment geared to the needs and interest of the local population. The programmes it broadcasts will often reflect the region it covers. A radio station covering a rural, farming area with farming news, market prices and gardening talk shows will be very different in style, pace and approach to the station broadcasting to a big city because interests differ radically. A good station should be an image of its audience.

• Flexibility
A radio is portable and can be listened to anywhere, even when doing other things. A car driver cannot read a newspaper or watch television when driving to work but he can turn on the radio. Advertisements are usually quick and easy to produce and can be slotted in at very short notice. Your local radio station can write, record and transmit your advertisement within the space of a few hours. Radio, being live, immediate and topical will also add a sense of urgency and importance. In addition, your advertisements can be broadcasted to specific listening audiences either by region or by time of day. An advertisement for a market garden centre could be heard in all rural areas through different local radio stations during, for example, weekly gardening shows.

• Low cost
Airtime, especially when purchased in packages, is relatively inexpensive as is the writing and recording of advertisements. You could, therefore, afford to increase the length or frequency of your advertisements in order to constantly remind and re-inforce your message.

Disadvantages
Local radio does, unfortunately, have a number of drawbacks.

• Transience
Radio is a very brief and forgettable medium. Listeners do not tune in for advertisements and may mentally 'switch off' when they are on. Only a few outstanding advertisements will be remembered for any length of time. Unfortunately, little information can be transmitted in a short space of time and it cannot be retained, as it is often difficult for the listener to make a permanent record. A car driver cannot, for example, write

down an address or telephone number. A radio advertisement cannot be returned to, because in seconds it is gone.

• Invisible

The radio is totally dependent on sound for the success of its message. Unlike other media it cannot offer a picture, text, colour, movement, an ability to demonstrate or a permanent record. If the script is weak, the voice irritates, overwhelms, or is too persistent, or even if the quality of reception is poor, then the message fails.

• Low listening figures

This is very much a secondary medium, with the small number of potential customers in relation to other media such as television. To reach a wide range and quantity of listeners advertisements need to be constantly repeated at different times of the day. Such intensive advertising can be expensive and, for the regular listener, repetition could be boring and have a negative effect. Even during the peak 6.00 am to 9.00 am period, the number of listeners actively listening to an advertisement is only a small percentage of those with radios switched on. A BBC survey published in 1978 indicated that between 7.30 am and 8.30 am only 5 per cent of those people with a radio on actually listened to it.

• Difficult to measure success

It is often difficult to research local radio audiences. In addition, it is difficult for you to measure response because it is a one dimensional, transient medium. The listener cannot return a coupon or free post envelope and you have to rely on asking your customers if they heard the advertisement.

Outdoor and Transportation Advertising

The town and country planning regulations state that outdoor advertising is 'any word, letter, model, sign, placard, board, notice, device or representation, whether illuminated or not, used for the purpose of advertisement, announcement or direction. It includes any hoarding or similar structure used or adapted for the display of advertisements'.

Characteristics

Outdoor advertising generally takes the form of posters of differing size, shape and content mounted on hoardings, billboards, information panels or bus shelters alongside pave- ments, main roads or around shopping centres. It is, however, a diverse medium and can even include stickers on litter bins or meters. Transportation advertising includes posters of varying size on or inside buses, taxis, trains, tube trains or in railway stations, tube stations, waiting rooms, forecourts or booking offices.

Posters will, depending on their location, be specifically used to either 'remind' or 'inform'. Outdoor advertisements are generally used to remind, as they are usually seen very briefly by a busy passerby who can only take in a short, sharp message. These advertisements should be seen frequently, demand attention by being big and bold and must be easy to read and understand.

Transport advertisements generally inform; they are read by travellers waiting for buses, trains or tube trains. Such advertisements may be lengthier and more detailed because the traveller remaining on the bus or train will have the time to complete the 'read'; thus, you have what could be termed a captive audience.

The market

The audience for outdoor advertisers is potentially high. As 80 per cent of the population live in urban areas, posters are, therefore, seen by almost everybody on a regular basis. The correct location of posters will ensure that they are seen, time and again, by your target market. For example, posters around shopping centres or precincts will attract housewives and shoppers; billboards on main roads will be seen by drivers; trains, tube trains and stations are ideal locations for advertising to business executives and office workers; buses are good for advertising car accessories to drivers travelling behind or cigarettes and tobacco to smokers travelling on the top deck. Different sites attract different types of consumers and the medium is so flexible and extensive that you can pinpoint and advertise to a precise market.

Advantages

Outdoor and transportation advertising offers the benefits of:

• Visibility

Posters are generally big and bold, they occupy dominant positions and are eye catching and colourful. They are attractive, full of impact and real, and are on display twenty-four hours each day for at least a month, with many companies renting sites on a semi-permanent basis. As such, they have long life and good exposure. The target audience will see them again and again, which will remind and reinforce your message. The secret of successful advertising is, of course, repetition.

Moving advertisements, i.e. on buses and taxis, have an added advantage in that they are being seen constantly by an increasing audience.

• Goodwill

Informative posters in particular, on railway, tube and bus stations generate goodwill and interest. When passengers are waiting for a bus or train it provides them with something to occupy their time and relieve the boredom. In such a situation, you can impact detailed information, for even if the passenger has not had time to read it all today, he will be able to finish it off tomorrow when he is once again waiting for his bus or train.

• Flexibility

Posters offer you flexibility and versatility. Approximately 50 per cent of all sites change hands each year, offering a greater choice of location. You can advertise nationally, regionally or even locally on just one specific site or, alternatively, choose buses, trains or stations on specific routes. You may decide to advertise on the tube line that brings passengers to your doorstep or on buses that pass by your door every day. Posters are available in a number of different sizes from 'double crowns' (30 × 20 inches) through to 'supersites' (96 feet × 45 feet) according to your needs and budget and can advertise your products for a month or a number of years. The most popular size of poster is 'four sheets' (40 × 60 inches).

Disadvantages

Posters do have several drawbacks.

• A busy audience

With many posters, people passing by have very little time to stop and read. Usually they are driving to work, hurrying to do the shopping or picking the children up from school, thus reducing the span of concentration, taking in little information. Posters generally can only be used to remind and reinforce existing, well known products rather than inform and provide lengthier details on new ones. The 'Gold' Benson and Hedges cigarette posters are an excellent example of an advertisement which, at a glance, reminds people of an established product in a clever and amusing way.

• Easily damaged

In poor weather, posters are liable to fade or mark easily. Although they are regularly checked and replaced, it can still often obscure or detract from the message. Graffiti can similarly be harmful, especially if it's funnier than the original poster.

• Lengthy preparation

Campaigns have to be planned well in advance. From initial design through to posting can take as long as three months and with some sites unavailable for perhaps a further month or two, and a minimum contract of one month, it means that your message may need to be relevant for up to six months ahead. Also, you cannot readily alter your advertisement to meet sudden changes in the market, you must get it right first time.

The Cinema

As an advertising medium the cinema accounts for only 2 per cent of advertising expenditure in the UK. Nevertheless, it is a medium which many small advertisers can use effectively.

Characteristics

The cinema is in many ways the most complete medium of all. It offers the advertiser size, sound, pictures, colour, movement and the ability to demonstrate. By showing a wide range of films from Disney comedies to horror movies, the cinema provides the advertiser with a number of clearly defined and interested audiences.

The market

The cinema, as a result of the growth of television and video, is a medium in decline. A peak of 1,600 million visitors each year after the last war dropped to 127 million in 1978 and, 10 years later, to an estimated 62 million. Nowadays, 42 per cent of the population never go to the cinema and those who do visit less frequently. It is no longer a regular habit. Whilst you can advertise your goods or services to a specific audience, for example, children and their parents when the cinema shows Spielberg or Disney films, you also need to accept that this potential audience is a small and constantly reducing one.

The most regular cinemagoers are those in the 15 to 24 age group. Surveys indicate that they form an average of 65 per cent of any given cinema audience. Around 75 per cent of those in that age range visited the cinema in the last six months and around 40 per cent in the last month. The average cinemagoer of this age visits the cinema once every two months and around

50 per cent visit with a friend of the opposite sex. Only 6 per cent visit alone and the remainder tend to go in groups of the same sex. Males and females visit in equal numbers although, as might be expected, they show distinct preferences for different films, as do the different social grades. ABC1s prefer 'PG' or '15 certificate' films and C2DEs favour 'X' certificate, horror and adult movies.

Cinema is generally considered as a medium directed to and visited by young unmarried couples. Films tend to reflect their audiences and as few of today's films are aimed at children, housewives or pensioners, you should bear in mind that the potential target market is a narrow and limited one.

Advantages

The cinema has the following benefits:

- **Impact**

A huge, dominating screen with sound, colour and action creates a strong and lasting impression on the audience. Research has shown that 50 per cent of cinemagoers can recall seven days later not only the name of a product or company, but also specific details of their advertisement as well.

- **Attention**

The advertisement will be seen in an ideal environment. It has a captive, attentive audience in a darkened room with ' no interruptions or distractions. The audience wants to be there and is ready and willing to absorb your message.

- **Flexibility**

You can choose to advertise for just one week in one local cinema or select specific towns on a regional or national basis. You may, for example, wish to advertise purely in seaside towns or in an upper or lower social area. If you wish you can advertise for several months on an 'alternative week campaign' (one week on, one week off) or even over several years. You can even advertise alongside specific films related in some way to your business or alongside a series of films. Rank, for example, can offer the advertiser a Disney package, should he wish to reach an audience of younger children and their parents. Whatever your choice, your advertisement will usually be shown in a ten minute sequence prior to the main feature, and as an added bonus, will not be shown at the same time as a competitor's. It is a first class solus position.

Disadvantages

The cinema has several drawbacks.

● Small, limited audiences
The characteristic make up of the modern audience limits the range of goods and services that can be advertised. A visit to your local cinema will reveal that the majority of advertisements are for 'teen' goods such as jeans, fashion, drinks. Products and services for families meet with little success because, unlike television, this is not a family orientated medium.

● Repetition
The dwindling number of potential customers at each showing means that your advertisement will need to be repeated constantly to be seen by the same number of potential customers as advertisements in other media. This can be costly and, to regular cinemagoers, can have negative value. They may be bored or, in groups, may actually barrack the film. Advertisements that are amusing when first seen can irritate the second or third time around. Remember, a teenage audience is notoriously fickle and hard to please.

● Transient
As with television and radio, cinema is a transient medium which relies heavily on visual impact, humour and jingles to succeed. It can rarely explain or provide details and, being brief, must make a very quick impression. Also, it cannot provide the viewer with a record for future reference.

5
Below the Line

Direct Mail

Direct mail is a specialised and precise form of advertising. It may be defined as postal advertising, whereby personally addressed mail is sent directly to an identified customer via the postal service. It is from distinct 'mail drops' where general, unaddressed 'junk' mail is hand delivered on a door-to-door basis.

Characteristics

Direct mail falls into four categories:

1. A 'direct campaign' makes an offer to the potential customer and will usually include a brochure or catalogue with a price list, order form and a reply envelope.
2. An 'informative campaign' is designed to educate the potential customer about your product or service and will normally include detailed product literature.
3. A 'reminder campaign' will follow up earlier mailings.
4. 'Utility direct mail' is the name given to supporting material such as calenders, charts and samples which may also be incorporated in some or all campaigns.

Whatever type of campaign is chosen, you need firstly to identify the actual prospects you wish to approach since this medium is designed to target known individuals rather than larger, more general groups of people as other forms of media do. Therefore, you will need to acquire a list of names and addresses for potential customers. There are four basic types of list:

1. 'In house lists' are those compiled from your own records of past or present customers.

2. 'Off the shelf lists' are those which you can compile yourself from directories or membership lists of appropriate organisations.

3. A 'managed list' is owned by a mailing house or company who will regularly check and update it, renting it out on a 'one use only' basis. You can approach a professional direct mail house to rent or buy their lists.

4. 'Broker lists' are available from list brokers who will choose, mix and even build a specific list for a particular advertiser.

The market

Over 800 million items of direct mail are delivered through the Post Office to households each year and over 400 million to business addresses. It is estimated that 93 per cent of businesses and 75 per cent of householders are happy to receive direct mail, when the subject matter is of interest. Approximately 81 per cent of business people generally read direct mail, compared to 62 per cent of householders.

Direct mail is ideal for those businesses who have a specialised, relatively small target market which can easily be identified. 'The market' could be anything from every shopkeeper in a local town who belongs to the Chamber of Trade, to all new homeowners on a particular estate who may want double glazing. It is not a medium suited to large scale, mass advertising where the expense of approaching each person individually would not be cost effective, unless you have the specialised production and mailing facilities in-house. Chapter 10 deals with this matter in more detail.

Advantages

Direct mail offers the benefits of:

● **Selectivity**
You can appeal directly to specific, known individuals, selecting

as many or as few as you need on a local or national basis. A shopfitter, for example, could approach every shop manager in a town or each toy shop manager of a particular chain of shops across the country. The medium is precise and specific and as long as your list is accurate and 'clean', you can obtain complete coverage of your target market with very little wastage. No list can ever give you 100 per cent redemption; however, careful targeting and a well presented package can increase your redemption from 0.5 per cent to 6 per cent.

• Individuality
Direct mail is a personally addressed medium. Each letter, addressed specifically to Mr Jones or Mrs Smith is private, appears to be individual and therefore special. Such a personal letter, if well written, should have a positive effect on the receiver provided the receiver has not been saturated before with such mail. They will then be able to give the letter their full attention. With such positive feelings you will be more likely to ensure that your message convinces them to buy the product or service on offer.

• Flexibility
This medium is very flexible. A campaign can, if necessary, be arranged swiftly with a sales letter written, printed and despatched in the same day. You can time mail shots to a specific season, month, week or day. For example, the financial consultant can arrange for Mr Smith to receive his letter immediately after Budget day when he may be confused and slightly worried about his future finance. Small, select groups can be advertised to, a little at a time, perhaps testing copy or supplying a slightly different message to each individual or to your entire target market in one shot. You can time reminders to suit your requirements and budget.

• Enclosures
You can send a single letter or include leaflets, brochures, catalogues, price lists, prepaid reply envelopes or even free samples, to attract and interest the potential customer. As much

or as little information as is desired can be sent in a format of your choice. A direct mail letter plus the appropriate enclosures is already one step ahead of the other media. The customer does not need to make any effort to obtain details of products or prices because all the necessary information is to hand and the enclosed freepost envelope and order form make ordering easy too.

• Control
As indicated, your advertising can easily be controlled, mailing when and where you wish. It is easy to check the success rate by the volume and value of replies and, if necessary, the campaign can be adjusted accordingly.

• Long life
Direct mail material can be filed by the recipient and kept for future reference. It is permanent and intransient. For example, the use of wall charts and calenders will keep your business permanently on display in the customer's premises.

Disadvantages
There are, however, also several drawbacks to direct mail:

• Mailing lists
An advertising campaign can only be as good as its mailing list. These may be difficult to obtain or, more likely, may be inaccurate. People die, move away, change jobs or simply lose interest in a particular hobby. A man who has purchased sports equipment in the past may no longer be in the marketplace because he is now too old to continue playing.

• Cost
A campaign can be expensive, especially if lists are not scrupulously accurate and shots are wasted. Stationery, catalogues, leaflets, brochures, postage and reply paid envelopes are all costly. Appropriate literature also takes time and expertise to write, print and post.

● **Specialisation**

Few advertisers realise that direct mail is a very specialised medium which requires exceptionally high standards of skill and expertise to succeed. It is difficult to write good copy which will attract and interest the reader. A great deal of direct mail received will irritate and annoy. As a simple example, if John Davies receives a letter which begins 'Dear Mr Davies' he may well read on. A letter beginning 'Dear Mr Davis' or 'Dear Mr David' will immediately irritate him, as might 'Dear John', whilst a letter greeting him as 'Dear Sir or Madam' will undoubtedly be consigned to the waste bin unread.

● **Inattention**

There is still an intellectual and social stigma attached to the idea of direct mail, and many people claim that they automatically throw it away. This is a disadvantage which can be overcome by the style and impact of a well produced, personalised and well presented direct mail package. (Remember, if you hold lists yourself then you must comply with the Data Protection Act.)

Exhibitions

As an advertising medium, exhibitions have increased in popularity to the stage where, today, most ambitious small advertisers regularly exhibit their goods and services. British companies currently spend over £300 million each year exhibiting in locations as diverse as a caravan in a local car park to a custom built stand at Earls Court, Olympia or the National Exhibition Centre.

Characteristics

There are many different types of exhibitions and the smaller business can choose one to suit its needs and budget. Shows can be held indoors in hotels, libraries, halls or exhibition centres. If goods or services are bulky or need room for demonstration, exhibitions may be held more effectively in open air venues such as Sandown Park and Crystal Palace. The Air Show at Farnborough and The Royal Show at the National Agricultural Centre are examples of major outdoor exhibitions.

Shows can be staged for the public (consumer exhibitions) such as the Ideal Home Exhibition or for trade only (trade exhibitions) such as Business Efficiency or Direct Marketing Fair. Some, such as the Motor Show or Boat Show are held for both the public and trade visitors, with separate days being allocated for each.

The majority of these exhibitions are run by trade associations or sponsored by well known organisations. For example, the Society of Motor Manufacturers and Traders runs the Motor Show and *The Daily Mail* lends its name to the Ideal Home Exhibition. Others are arranged by professional organisers such as IPS Exhibitions Limited, Industrial and Trade Fairs Limited or Maclaren Exhibitions Limited.

Many smaller advertisers, rather than exhibit once or twice each year at expensive exhibition centres, are choosing to run their own semi-permanent mobile or portable exhibitions. Here the exhibits are taken by road to local towns and quickly set up in car parks, at schools, hotels, libraries, fêtes or local shows.

The market

With exhibitions, the advertiser has a choice. You can exhibit in a large, national show such as the Ideal Home Exhibition and, assuming your site position is good, can reach a mass audience of differing ages and types. However, you must also bear in mind that it is likely that only a tiny percentage of those people attending will be interested in your products. Many visitors will merely be browsing around, helping themselves to free coffee, biscuits and expensive sales literature. In addition, there is still a lack of audience research for many exhibitions, with little or no information as to the number and type of visitor.

Attendance figures can be misleading. They do not mean that the more people there are attending, the more you will sell. How many people attending the Motor Show will actually go out and buy a new car?

On the other hand, you may prefer to exhibit to a high quality, ticket-only audience, where fewer people may attend but those who do will tend to be potential buyers. Trade, sports and hobby shows, by invitation only, will ensure a high calibre of visitor. Also visitor application forms will give you not only details of the market, but a ready made mailing list for a direct mail follow up campaign.

Advantages

Exhibitions have many benefits for the advertiser:

• Personal contact
It is an ideal way of meeting a large number of clients and potential clients, in one central location. It is very convenient. You can personally see more clients in one day than you could in a week on the road. There is a relaxed and informal 'show' atmosphere in which you have the time to explain, inform and demonstrate. The customer can see, test and sample the product or service, which creates confidence and goodwill. You can benefit from the customer's reactions and feedback.

• Sales
An exhibition can be used to improve present and future business. Goods can actually be sold on the stand or orders be taken. In addition, new products or services can be launched, judged and modified. It is an excellent way of testing the market.

• Catalogues
The visitor, public or trade, will be supplied with or will buy an exhibition catalogue detailing each exhibitor. This will some-times be available prior to the show or will be read on the journey to and from it. Most visitors will keep it as a source of reference on a semi-permanent basis, or at least until the exhibition takes place again the following year. It provides a written, intransient record of you, the advertiser.

● **Status**

For many companies an exhibition is a way of maintaining reputation and status within the trade. It is important to 'put on a show' because so many businesses exist and thrive on their reputation that they must 'keep up with the Joneses'. An exhibition does, of course, have great publicity value. It is in people's thoughts for many weeks, is a talking point in the trade and can be newsworthy – especially if a dramatic new product is unveiled for the first time.

Disadvantages

Exhibitions do also have several drawbacks:

● **Cost**

They can be very expensive to mount. The stand needs to be designed and built, decorated, fitted and furnished. The site must be paid for and, if it is in a good location, it is expensive. In addition, running costs are high. Bills for electricity, the printing of leaflets, catalogues, price lists, the cost of hospitality and insurance all have to be met. Staff will have to be taken away from their normal jobs to host the exhibition, tying up valuable time and with a potential for lost sales from regular sources. In some instances they will also need to be accommodated and fed. The total cost involved is, for many smaller businesses, prohibitive, especially at the large, professionally run exhibitions which take place at major venues.

● **Competition**

Exhibitions have a common theme and, as such, the exhibitors are, to a varying extent, in competition with each other. In other media you can advertise on your own and you have the customers' attention. At a show you are fighting for it with a dozen other companies.

● **Attendance**

Smaller shows in smaller venues are often poorly publicised and attendances are affected accordingly. In addition, there can be very little information pre- or post-show, about the attendance and the type of visitors. It is difficult, therefore, to judge whether a show is suitable for your business unless you actually take a stand and find out the hard way whether or not it is an expensive mistake or a viable selling aid.

Sales Promotion

Sales promotion is the universal title given to all the different types of promotional exercises that take place, quite often at the point of sale. It plays an important role in the advertising process because it can remind a potential customer of a product or service at the very moment they are ready and willing to buy. Research has estimated that over £4,000 million is spent on sales promotion in one form or another each year.

Characteristics

Sales promotion can take the form of free gifts, where a comb may be given away with a bottle of shampoo; free samples, where the customer can try a trial sachet of shampoo or baby food; or cash inducements such as money off vouchers or cash dividends. Manufacturers will also offer gifts or cash on a 'mail in' basis, where the customer must collect and send a certain number of pack coupons. This and picture cards such as those given with PG Tips Tea, promote a regular collecting habit.

Another popular method of attracting customers and advertising a product or service is to provide the retailer with either 'point of sale' material or sales literature. Point of sale material is designed for windows, doors, shelves, counters and floors and includes posters and stickers, stands, models, dump bins and mobiles. It can even include items such as ashtrays, mats, carrier bags and door signs. Access and Barclaycard, for example, produce excellent 'Open/Closed' signs often used by retailers; which ensure that the first and last thing the customer sees is the credit card logo.

Sales literature can also be used to provide detailed and

permanent information. This will normally take the form of catalogues, leaflets, brochures, folders, price lists, wall charts and calenders.

The market

Clearly the market is wide and diverse, with promotions in supermarkets, shops, cafés, restaurants and garages – anywhere a person can buy a product or service. You can obviously direct your advertising to a precise target market. For instance, the manufacturer of car accessories can provide window stickers to garages and petrol stations and the publisher can provide bookshops with a display stand. Both know that their point of sale material will catch the eye of the target audience.

Each individual form of sales promotion has its own specific advantages and disadvantages. There are, however, a number of points which most have in common.

Advantages

• Reminder
Sales promotion has a major and significant advantage over other media in that, when it is seen, the customer is already in the shop and in a buying mood. If you can catch their attention it will require little effort for them to make a purchase.

• Popular
Many promotions are very popular and are seen as fun or exciting. The product sold with free picture cards will be bought again and again because it is enjoyable to collect the cards and stick them in a book. Also, it is exciting to collect coupon halves from petrol stations to see if they will match, winning you a major prize.

Disadvantages

Sales promotion has a number of drawbacks:

• Wasteful

In the vast majority of schemes, material and literature is simply wasted. It has been estimated that up to 90 per cent of all point of sale material is never used. The retailer will select, often from a considerable choice, the most suitable products for his shop and the rest, however excellent in idea or quality, will be discarded.

A manufacturer may produce the brightest and most colourful display stand but if it is too large for the retailer's limited space, or is the wrong colour, it will not be used. In addition, many retailers dislike handling coupons or other schemes because of the extra work involved. Sales promotion should, therefore, also be geared to the needs of the retailer.

• Short life

Many schemes are of little use because they have a limited lifespan. Some promotional ideas are seasonal. The display stand shaped like a Christmas tree is of use for only a few short weeks and the boxes of cereal which promote a free barbecue in return for coupons will not sell once the summer has passed. A short lifespan and potential wastage makes the cost of planning, producing and distributing a sales promotion prohibitive for many smaller companies.

• Market saturation

There are so many schemes and offers available that customers tend to pick and choose items because of the particular promotion. They lose brand loyalty, shopping around for the right offer rather than the right brand. Other customers may find it boring – 'not another special offer' – and view the product with contempt because it may appear that it needs a free gift in order to sell.

• Response

It is often very difficult to prejudge the response to a promotion and this can result in delays in supplying goods. Such delays will lead to illwill and dissatisfaction if the customer has spent time and money collecting, cutting and sending coupons. Perhaps the most famous example of this problem was the free lighter offer from John Players cigarettes in 1980. Players anticipated a take-up of between 3,000 and 5,000 but actually had to distribute over 2 million free lighters. So beware, 'cast your bread upon the waters' and you may get only a ripple or be engulfed by a tidal wave.

6
Choosing the Best Medium

In order to succeed, you need to make the correct choice and use the available media. If you do not advertise through the right medium at the right time to the right people, then your campaign, however brilliant and imaginative the idea, will probably fail.

To ensure that you achieve this objective, you will have to evaluate and compare the media in the following areas before making your final decisions.

Form

It is important to consider the form of a particular medium and whether the advertisement will be watched, read or listened to. Clearly, some forms are more advantageous to certain products or services than others. For example, the manufacturer selling to other companies, which wishes to provide precise and detailed information, would probably choose a reading medium such as specialist newspapers, magazines or direct mail. The advertiser for a company selling soft drinks to children and teenagers, who seeks to remind with a humorous, zippy slogan may prefer a watching or listening medium such as the cinema or radio. A company advertising a new, colourful toy will seek a medium which offers colour and, if the toy is complicated, will also look for a medium which offers the opportunity to demonstrate (e.g. television).

Each advertiser, depending on his product or service, must choose a form that will attract the most attention and lead to maximum sales.

Timing

You must decide on the most effective time for an advertising campaign. For some advertisers, it may be a choice of different seasons. Summer goods (e.g. garden furniture) generally sell in the summer and winter goods (e.g. car radiator anti-freeze) in winter. Alternatively, it may be more important to choose the right month. The owner of a number of holiday homes will advertise more successfully in January, when people are thinking about a summer holiday. If you manufacture novelty items for Christmas you will need to advertise to your trade customers in the first part of the year to ensure your goods reach the shops in time for the Christmas season. For other advertisers, it may be a choice of a particular week or day, perhaps even morning or evening. The advertiser who sells household items may wish to time his radio advertisements to reach housewives in the morning before they do the shopping. An off licence may aim to appeal to businessmen on their way home from work in the hope that they will buy beer or wine for consumption that evening.

Availability

Linked to timing is the question of availability. Is the right medium available at the right time? The holiday homes owner seeking to advertise in January may not be able to if his 'right' medium, a holiday brochure, was fully booked six months earlier. The Christmas novelty manufacturer may find that the appropriate trade press has been inundated with other manufacturers selling the same type of seasonal goods and has already sold all its available advertising space.

Unless campaigns are planned well in advance, it may not be possible to choose the right space or site at the right time. Poster sites are usually taken on a long term, semi-permanent basis and exhibition stands are quite regularly rebooked at the end of one exhibition for the next year's event.

In addition, certain media such as television or radio may be unwilling to take advertisements from companies that they consider to be 'unsuitable' advertisers, offering goods or services which might offend the majority of their viewers or listeners. Your chosen medium may be widely used by a major competitor and again this could also influence your choice. For example, if ten competitors advertise on the radio, you may be viewed as 'exclusive' if you make use of posters instead. On the other hand, the holiday homes owner could benefit from being grouped with others, listed under the resort heading of Torquay or Great Yarmouth in a newspaper, catching the reader in a receptive 'Where am I going to go?' mood.

Leadtimes

Another aspect of timing is that of leadtime. How long will it take for your advertisement to reach the target audience? You may, for example, need to wait for poster sites to become available. The billboard on the main route in and out of town may already be booked for some time ahead by the Tesco superstore two miles away and so you may have to wait several months for your poster to be put up.

You will also need to take into account the leadtime required by the medium you have selected. Copy for colour magazines, for instance, is usually needed several months before being published, whereas local radio and press can often accept material at short notice. A constantly changing business wishing to advertise a sale at short notice may not, therefore, be able to use its first choice medium.

Frequency

As an advertiser, you have to consider how frequently each medium appears. Media such as the radio, cinema or television can reach potential customers several times a day, the press daily, weekly or monthly, whereas exhibitions mainly take place just once a year. Consider too how frequently the advertising message can be changed. The press and radio can implement changes quickly, but changing a poster may take months.

Duration

The life of an advertisement in each medium is of some significance in the selection process. Television, cinema and radio are all transient media and the message is quickly gone and often forgotten. Press advertising, however, can last anything from ten minutes with a quickly discarded daily newspaper, to months or even years if, for example, magazines are kept for future reference.

The duration of response will be similar with, for example, a radio advertisement leading to immediate replies, while a magazine advertisement could still have some enquiries arriving several years later from distant parts of the world.

Cost

A comparison of media on the basis of cost alone is exceedingly difficult. Space, time and sites are all sold in different ways. Magazines are sold as a fraction of a page; newspapers by single column centimetre; cinema and radio in, say, 30, 45, or 60 second slots. In addition, there are obviously differing costs for different sizes and positions plus a host of package deals, discounts and inducements. On top of basic charges for space or time there are additional production costs to be considered. The rental of an exhibition stand may be relatively low but working expenses quickly add up. Posters need to be designed and printed and, even if you intend to have a poster on one site for one month, you will need several copies printed to allow for bad weather and vandalism. Many advertisers try to compare costs on a 'cost per thousand' basis, whereby the cost of reaching each thousand of the target market is based on, say, the price of a single column centimetre divided by the newspaper's circulation. For example, a newspaper which charges £1 per single column centimetre and has a circulation of 10,000, would mean a cost of £1 divided by 10 which equals 10 pence per thousand. A magazine might charge £5 per single column centimetre but with a circulation of 100,000, this would give a cost per thousand of only five pence. Clearly, an approximate comparison can be made for each medium to indicate which gives value for money. However, as previously stated, you should also look at circulation, readership or viewing figures with a healthy scepticism and bear in mind that however cost effective a medium may appear, the only true measure of success is the number of replies and, more importantly, the quantity of business eventually obtained. A huge television campaign, at a lower cost per thousand than direct mail, may be less successful – it may simply be the wrong medium for your product.

Audience

In choosing media, it is important to research the audience they reach. As indicated in Chapter 3 audited estimates of circulation readership, viewing and listening figures are available from both media owners and independent analysts such as BARB and JICNARS. Figures can be used for comparison, but the potential advertiser should bear in mind that they are often dated and occasionally suspect. Remember also that statistics, even accurate ones, can be manipulated. Even genuine figures can be misleading or unhelpful. For example, weekly or monthly figures are often quoted giving no indication of which days are good or bad. The total number of exhibition visitors may not take into account those going in and out two, three or even four times. A poster may have hundreds of potential customers passing by each morning on their way to the nearby railway station but, if it's raining and many have umbrellas, few will actually see it and absorb the message.

Profile

Clearly, the quality of those seeing the advertisement is of far greater importance than the quantity. The media profile indicating audience composition in terms of sex, type, age and social grade, should closely match that of your target market. For example, the profile of a magazine such as *Harpers and Queen* is likely to be almost 100 per cent female and, as such, is an ideal medium for advertising goods such as women's clothes, perfume and make up.

In addition, the profile can be divided into age groups where, for example, *Cosmopolitan* may be read by younger women, with *Homes & Gardens* being read by older women. Similarly, *Cosmopolitan* may have a high AB profile in comparison to a high C2DE profile for *The People's Friend.*

Penetration

Consider also how far each medium penetrates into a particular market. The manufacturer of a small range of toys who wishes to advertise for stockists may find that a specialised trade magazine such as *Toy Trader* has a relatively small and limited circulation, but it will reach a high proportion of the potential market. Quality is better than quantity. The cinema may have low viewing figures in relation to television but for the advertiser of teenage goods, the message will achieve greater penetration of the target market with a lower level of wastage.

Mood

Trying to assess the mood of the media customer is a fascinating and often impossible task. The customer's mood will, however, affect the success of your advertising message. An advertisement may be perceived as intrusive, acceptable or, if read or seen at the right time, of interest. For example, the viewer watching a favourite film on television may see an advertisement as an irritating intrusion, whereas a businessman attending a trade show is likely to be receptive and interested in receiving the advertising message.

It will sometimes be the case that you will need to choose more than one medium to successfully advertise your goods or services.

A primary medium might, for example, be chosen for initial impact and a secondary medium selected to repeat and remind the target market. A local shopkeeper may choose his local radio or newspaper as a primary medium and support this with a series of reminder posters around town. A small manufacturer may advertise for stockists through the trade press and support this campaign with the use of direct mail, sales literature and point of sale material. The important thing is to remain flexible and make use of the particular medium which offers the best opportunities at any given point in time.

7
Getting Your Message Across

There are many ways of conveying a sales message through an advertising medium, including the use of:

- Humour.
- Slogans and jingles.
- Emotion.
- Presenters.
- Demonstration.
- Comparison.

Humour

Humour can be an impressive and powerful sales aid. Witty advertising, slogans or jingles can soften a hard sales message and ensure it is absorbed by the customer in a pleasant and relaxed atmosphere. Many advertisers believe that to be actively seen and remembered, an advertisement needs to be entertaining. It is true that surveys have shown that the public do find humorous advertisements to be the most enjoyable and memorable. Advertisements for such products as Heineken, Carling Black Label, Hamlet and PG Tips have all, through the use of humour, captured the public's imagination and have even become a topic of everyday conversation and jokes. Even the most unlikely products can benefit from a humorous approach. Volkswagen and Sony have both, perhaps surprisingly, used it to great effect.

Advertisers in any media can approach a campaign in a

humorous manner. For example, the radio is ideal for creating humorous and imaginative situations. For some time, Mel Smith and Griff Rhys Jones ran a series of highly successful advertisements for Philips. Radio also works well utilising music to produce humorous verse such as the butter advertisement that promises 'You'll never put a better bit of butter on your knife'. Cinema, offering both sound and vision, can supply many humorous stock films. A popular and widely used example is for opticians. It shows a bespectacled man staggering blindly into every shop in the street except the local optician who would, of course, be able to supply him with the perfect pair of spectacles. Posters can also be effective. One of the most famous is the 1930s Pears Soap poster which showed a tramp writing to the company to thank them for their soap and promising that, from now on, he will use no other. Such an advertisement would lend itself equally well to use in the press, on point of sale material or even in direct mail. Figure 7.1 shows a humorous approach to selling a specialised toilet soap.

However, you do need to consider that each individual viewer, listener or reader will view humour in different ways. The man who slips on a banana skin and falls flat on his face will raise a tremendous laugh with some, a smile with others but leave a good number wholly unmoved. Subtle or offbeat humour may have the same affect. Humour which does not hit its target can obscure or negate the sales message. It may even provoke an adverse reaction if it is seen as being crude or unfunny. Advertisements involving 'alternative' comedians to attract younger customers could also alienate all but a narrow segment of the population. In addition, some humour is so funny and successful that it is what the viewer remembers, not the product. For example, you will recall the highly popular Leonard Rossiter and Joan Collins advertisements, but how many of you can remember the name of the drink they were advertising?

Finally, some products and services are totally unsuitable for use with humour. A funeral director, for example, would have little success with a humorous campaign.

Some people are still old-fashioned enough to believe that cleanliness is next to godliness – and to put their faith completely in Cidal.

No soap is more effective than Cidal in banishing dirt from the skin; and, as it performs this worthy task, it gently removes – through a special hygiene ingredient – the bacteria that can lead not only to perspiration odour but to skin infection.

Cidal is kind to the skin both on the face and on the body. Indeed, it's so safe and effective, you'll find it widely used in hospitals.

Next time you're at the wash-basin or in the bath, let's hope it's with a bar of Cidal.

Otherwise you may wind up somewhat uncleaner than you should be.

And that might leave you less than amused.

Cidal. You won't find a more effective soap.

Reproduced by kind permission of Cidal Soap

Figure 7.1 A humorous, eye-catching advertisement.

Slogans and Jingles

Slogans and jingles often develop from humorous situations with 'I bet he drinks Carling Black Label' and 'Heineken refreshes the parts other beers cannot reach' being two prime examples. They are usually witty, amusing or topical. Ideally, they are short, catchy, memorable and repeat the brand name. 'Ah Bisto!' and 'Don't just book it, Thomas Cook it' are both excellent examples. Jingles, if the music is catchy, can stick in the listener's mind for days and, in a way, make a transient medium intransient.

All types of media are appropriate for the use of either jingles or slogans. Slogans can be printed on point of sale material, in the press, in direct mail and particularly on posters where the larger size will allow increased impact and act as a forceful reminder. Jingles can be spoken or sung on radio, in the cinema, on television and even on an exhibition stand.

You should, however, bear in mind a number of drawbacks. They can be too successful to the point where they, and not the product, are remembered. For example 'Nice one Cyril' became an everyday phrase in the early 1970s, but who remembers the name of the product? An additional problem is that a slogan can also become dated and boring. The reader or listener may mentally switch off the rest of the message because he thinks he has heard it all before. Jingles, of course, can stay in the consumer's mind for days but instead of reinforcing the sales message they merely become an irritant and have exactly the opposite effect.

Emotion

A great many advertisements rely on an emotional response from the viewer, listener or reader. For example, the government made use of shock and fear tactics to educate the public on drink/driving, the use of seatbelts and more recently Aids and contraception. Commercial advertisers, of course, must comply with the IBA and ASA guidelines that 'advertisements must not, without justifiable reason, play on fear', but they can still appeal to a customer's other emotions. Advertisements such as Hovis and Ovaltine have played on feelings of nostalgia and car advertisements often appeal to a customer's ego and desire for status. Pears Soap using a little girl, Andrex Toilet Tissue with its puppy and Pampers Disposable Nappies with its appealing toddlers all play on our feelings. Cigarette manufacturers try to generate a macho male image. Emotion can be used to great effect in most media and can be geared to suit the advertiser's particular product or service. The owner of a shoe repair business could use nostalgia – 'Shoes repaired by hand in the old fashioned way'. Similarly, a chocolate manufacturer could advertise 'Real chocolate – just like Grandma used to eat'. They could also extend the theme to include old fashioned wrappers, sales literature and press advertisements, to create a corporate nostalgic image.

Some media and types of business are ill suited to the use of emotion. It is difficult, if not impossible, to convey emotion in a press advertisement. There is insufficient room to develop a theme and the mood of reader at the time the advertisement is read may be completely wrong. Similarly, a financial institution would be better advised to appeal through logic and rational argument, rather than appealing to the emotions.

Presenters

A presenter is sometimes used to help sell a product through an advertising medium and many advertisers will try to attract a national or local celebrity to do this, although it can prove very expensive. A presenter, however, need not be a star or even a local household name. She may be unknown, perhaps a model chosen for her eyes, skin, teeth or hair. A shampoo manufacturer, for instance, would choose a model with beautiful, shiny, well groomed hair. A presenter can even be a puppet or cartoon character. For instance, you could have a local artist design a cartoon character to help promote your goods. Such a character could be used in advertisements and even for visiting local shops, stores and fêtes.

Presenters are also used to demonstrate a product. For example, in the television advertisements a 'housewife' shows viewers how to use carpet fresheners and household cleaners. Getting the presenter to interview satisfied customers is a technique frequently employed, particularly in washing powder and margarine advertisements. Well known personalities are often used to endorse a particular product through personal recommendation. Nescafé have used this to advantage in their advertisement with personalities such as Sarah Greene. (See Figure 7.2.)

The use of a presenter has a number of benefits in all media. It can give the product life and personality and help to make it memorable. It also adds status. If an authoritative voice on the radio says a product is good then many listeners will take note of it. The use of a celebrity will also link the product with their perceived qualities. For example, Nanette Newman who presents the Fairy Liquid advertisements is seen by most viewers as being a good wife and mother as well as a film actress. This helps to reinforce the product's image of being an effective household product with an added touch of glamour – it keeps your hands feeling as soft as your face! Also, each time that celebrity is seen in another guise it will serve to jog the customer's memory.

There are, of course, also drawbacks in using a presenter. One who is too well known may obscure your sales message or a cartoon character may eventually become more interesting than the product. A particular presenter may irritate or annoy some people and a celebrity's image in the eyes of the public can change if some scandal suddenly breaks in the Sunday newspapers. Unless you can agree an exclusive contract with a celebrity, which will undoubtedly cost a considerable amount of money, they could agree to advertise on behalf of other companies, diluting the strength of your product's link with them.

Demonstration

Demonstrating a product is widely used in advertising and can

Reproduced by kind permission of Nescafé and Sarah Greene

Figure 7.2 Use of a well-known presenter in a successful advertisement.

be very powerful and dramatic. For instance, a car can show its toughness and reliability driving across rough terrain. Look at the dramatic and inventive Peugeot advertisement showing their latest model driving alongside a blazing cane field. You can use demonstration across a wide range of products from a food processor chopping up vegetables to a strength test showing the holding power of a particular brand of super glue.

Obviously, demonstrating a product in this way is much more effective in media such as cinema or an exhibition. However, it can be used in print because a great deal of demonstration advertising will show off the product's appearance or its consumer benefits. A poster or press advertisement, for example, could show a beautifully cooked packet meal designed to make the reader's mouth water, or, in an advertisement for sun-tan lotion, an alluring bronzed body.

Demonstration on its own is rarely used to sell a product. Normally, it will be linked with other creative ideas such as product comparison. A good example of this was the Qualcast lawnmower advertisement which demonstrated both the Qualcast and Flymo machines mowing a lawn and then compared them by saying 'The Qualcast Concorde. It's a lot less bovver than a hover!'.

Comparison

Comparing your product or service to others is an increasingly popular method of advertising used in all media. You will be aware of many examples, especially in the motor industry, where 'knocking' copy is quite normal.

Such an approach has benefits if your product is genuinely superior. However, you would be well advised to limit your comments to broad generalisations rather than specific attacks on named competitors. Inaccurate and misleading observations can lead to costly legal proceedings, so it is wise to be cautious. Even if your comments are fair, you are still giving free publicity to your competitor and reminding the public about their products. The public may, as a result, buy their goods instead of yours. They may think your campaign is unfair, unpleasant and unethical and decide they do not wish to do business with a company who resorts to such tactics.

It is a good basic rule of thumb to concentrate on your own product and its benefits. Keep a watchful eye on your competitor but do not become involved in a slanging match or obsessed with what he is doing.

As with all the other ingredients which help to make up a successful advertising 'mix', vary the approach in line with the product or service being advertised. Be prepared to alter your style if initial results show that it is not working as you envisaged.

8
Creation and Design

Creating the Press Advertisement

Creating a really effective advertisement for newspapers or magazines can be difficult. Rules can be given but they do not guarantee success. They are often there to be broken and those who ignore them will probably succeed or fail in the same proportions as those who follow them to the letter.

There are, nevertheless, a few guidelines which you will need to consider concerning the layout and text of an advertisement. Layout should attract attention with the use of good headlines, illustrations and typography. Your advertisement should look co-ordinated, have a focal point and emphasise important points. Copy should be brief, logical, positive, repetitious and stylish.

Layout
Layout should:

- **Attract attention**
To succeed an advertisement must be seen. It can attract attention in many ways. You may choose a large advertisement which will stand out on the page and look impressive. This will also allow you to be creative or to provide extra information. However, do also take into account the fact that a large advertisement may be wasteful, will be expensive and may not be as successful as a series of smaller advertisements at the same cost. They will repeat and remind, which your single large advertisement will not.

An unusual shape or position may ensure the advertisement catches the eye. A triangular or circular one will undoubtedly stand out on a page of rectangles. An advertisement on the front or back cover will be seen by more people than those located inside. Every reader sees the cover, even if they do not read every page. A solus position, where the advertisement is the only one on a particular page, will contrast with the surrounding text and be away from any direct competition. Goods advertised on a specific page, e.g. sports or fashion page, will attract more readers so long as the product concerned is appropriate.

Colour, especially in a predominantly black and white section, will stand out. It will be more lifelike and appealing and will aid pack recognition. The goods in a colour advertisement will look just like they do in the shop. In a colour magazine, the use of strong, vibrant colours will probably be more effective than soft pastel shades.

The reader will also be attracted to a headline, an illustration or even the typography.

• Headlines

A headline can make or break an advertisement. It is often the first thing that catches the reader's eye and helps him to decide if he will read the rest of the text. Market research has indicated that five times as many people read a headline as actually read the text. It should, therefore, be able to sell the product or service on its own. There are many types of headline and no hard and fast rules exist about which are good or bad. To reiterate, they should catch the eye, hold the attention and reflect the mood and style of the advertisement.

A headline can be humorous, for example, 'Heineken refreshes the parts ...' works well with 'before' and 'after' illustrations and no copy. It may also be dramatic or interrogative. 'Seventy of your hairs will drop out today. How are you looking after the rest of them?' was a successful advertisement for a shampoo manufacturer. The headline may be declarative or comprise a testimonial – 'Probably the best lager in the world'. Here again this type of headline can also be linked with an interrogative approach – Gary Lineker and Ruth Madoc asking 'Do you insist on Walkers Crisps?' is a good illustration.

Often the most successful headlines are those which are newsworthy, arouse curiosity or offer a benefit. Rolls Royce once ran an advertisement with the headline 'At 60 miles per hour the loudest noise in this new Rolls Royce comes from the electric clock' - newsworthy, curious, intriguing and offering a benefit – a quiet drive!

● **Illustrations**
A good illustration will help to convey your message and sell your goods and services. It will be attractive and can have great impact and appeal, supplying information and adding drama, excitement, humour or realism. A product which sells mainly because of its appearance can be illustrated to attract attention and reinforce recognition. The product's benefits can be shown. Weightwatchers, for example, advertise by illustrating a success-ful slimmer with 'before' and 'after' photographs.

You can choose from several types of illustration, but they must be sharp, simple and relevant. Do not be too clever. A busy or obscure illustration will only detract from your sales message. Remember also to check the newspaper or magazine beforehand to ascertain the quality of reproduction.

When illustrating your advertisement use photographs which convey a sense of reality, or line drawings which are basically black sketches on a white background. This type of drawing can also be reversed out, i.e. white on black, or subtly shaded for additional effect. If you have a company logo reproduce it in your advertisement to enhance the company's image and help build customer recognition.

● **Typography**
Many advertisements, of course, do not use illustrations but rely wholly on the text for their success. Typography, the design and appearance of the print, is very important in such cases. The correct choice of typeface, size, density and layout will ensure that the text is legible, attractive and stylish. There are hundreds of different typefaces available and your printer or the selected medium will advise you on which are most suitable for your particular advertisement. It is important to select a design which

will suit your company's style and convey the correct mood. Copy face, for main text, should be small, closely set and easy to read. Display face, for headlines and headings, needs to be larger. Amongst the most popular typefaces your printer will show you are Garamond, Futura, Bembo, Goudy and Franklin Gothic.

Alternatively, you could choose a more classical typeface, developed from Roman characters, to give a more upmarket image. Perhaps you feel a more ornate or decorative typeface lends itself better to your product and house style. As with a line drawing, you can even select to have parts 'reversed out', with white type on a black background to make it stand out even more.

Each typeface will also be available in a number of point sizes and depths, i.e. shades, varying from light, extra light through medium to bold. Until you have acquired a reasonable working knowledge of typography, do not hesitate to seek advice and assistance from your printer or the production department of your chosen medium.

• Unity

Your advertisement must look co-ordinated and unified. It should be aesthetically pleasing and easy on the reader's eye, blending together to form a united whole. Text of different length and style, scattered at random around illustrations of different sizes, shapes and colours will jar the reader's eye and make them feel irritated.

• Focal point

Every advertisement should have a focal point around which the whole thing is built. For example, an advertisement for a new style of baby's pram would have an illustration of the product as the central point, with headlines and text laid out around it. Keep the advertisement clean and uncluttered. If the pram manufacturer decided to add a cute baby and various accessories to the illustration, the advertisement would be diluted and the impact and clarity of the original message lost. You can try to be too clever and sophisticated. What, you may ask, about the

'Gold' Benson and Hedges advertisements where it is sometimes difficult to even find the cigarette packet? (See Figure 8.1.) This only works because public awareness of the product and style of advertising is high. You would be better advised to keep your advertisements simple and straightforward.

● Emphasis

Severe regularity and layout can be boring. A little emphasis here and there provides variety and interest. Consider highlighting one section, the first paragraph perhaps, to attract attention and emphasise the main selling points. A contrast of light and dark text will be noticed but be careful not to emphasise too much. All emphasis is no emphasis – and it looks dreadful as well.

Copy

Copy should be:

● Brief

Text must be precise and concise, simple and easy to read. Points should be made clearly and be easy to understand and absorb. In particular, press advertisements are likely to remain unread if there is a mass of words. Large advertisements give you the time and space to explain and describe goods and services in detail but text should still be direct and to the point. Prepare your text and then be ruthless. Cut unnecessary words, sentences and paragraphs. They may be off putting and obscure your sales message. Use everyday words in simple sentences and short paragraphs. Remember, the average reader cannot absorb complex text or ideas.

● Logical

Text should be laid out in a logical and sensible manner. Headings and illustrations can be used to support and emphasise points. The correct use of grammar, punctuation, full stops and commas will give the text an easy-to-read rhythm. Consider your product or service from the potential buyer's

Reproduced by kind permission of Benson and Hedges

Figure 8.1
Detail from the Benson and Hedges 'Gold' advertisement.

viewpoint. He may not be interested in the selling points of the product as you see them. He wants to know what is in it for him. He probably will not want to know that the hi-fi is the first one imported into the country, that you have the region's biggest showroom or have been in business for thirty years. He may just be interested in the price. Decide what your customer perceives as the most important points and then tell him about them – and them alone. Be careful to close the copy at the right moment. Do not bore the customer. Leave him at a peak so that he wants to buy. Offer him an incentive – vouchers, coupons, discounts – for ordering by a certain date. *Which?* magazine regularly advertises three months free subscriptions to entice customers and offer extra consumer reports for replying within one or two weeks.

• Positive
Always make an advertisement positive and enthusiastic. Convey a sense of urgency and importance. 'Why not give us a call?' and 'Why not pop in?' should be replaced by the encouraging 'Call us Today!' and 'Call in Now!' You have the reader's attention so make the most of it.

• Repetitious
Often, only a small number of potential customers will see your advertisement. Few will want to read lengthy text and lists of advantages. As the advertiser, you should choose one major advantage or distinctive feature and repeat it. The reader can be distracted from, or bored by, endless copy but will be able to absorb one major buying point and retain it in his memory for some time.

• Non comparative
As previously mentioned, you would be ill advised to make direct comparisons between your product and that of a named competitor, however superior yours may be. If you invite comparison you should expect the consumer to also consider the other product. Should you have misjudged their criteria for buying, you could lose business.

- **Stylish**

Every advertisement should have a certain style and aim to be a little original. Write your copy, then read it back. Make sure it flows and is easy to read. Do try to be original. 'Come on down!' may seem a brilliant headline, but it has been used hundreds of times before. Try also to avoid clichés, corny expressions and trite phrases. A play on words can be successful. Perrier mineral water have had great success with their series of 'Eau' headlines above a picture of a bottle of their product – 'Eau la la', 'H2 Eau' and 'N'Eau Calories' being just a few examples.

Take care not to be too clever. Write copy as if you were talking, using everyday, conversational words that everyone understands. This may not, of course, be the case if you are writing advertising copy for a product or service being advertised in a professional or technical journal. In some ways, however, the principle will still apply in that the technical jargon will be part of the reader's everyday vocabulary. Avoid sounding pompous and superior. Any text which makes the reader feel you are talking down to him will merely cause offence and even alienation.

Creating a Good Radio Advertisement

Independent local radio stations do offer the advertiser a creation and production service, should this be needed. It is a facility, the cost of which is included within the package price detailed on the rate card, which is available directly from the station and through its sales agents. The service offers sound professional expertise and for most advertisers is a more viable proposition than hiring a separate studio and independent production experts, which would make the cost of the campaign prohibitive. Using your company's own sales literature and copies of advertisements in other media, the radio station will write and record a suitable advertisement for your business.

However, to ensure originality, you would be well advised to produce a number of ideas for your advertisement, which would then form the basis of a constructive discussion with the radio station's production department. You could also draft on tape a preliminary advertisement which would then be professionally remade by the station. After all, you know your business, products and market far better than a radio station. Your input is vital if you want an ideal advertisement which will put over your message and capture the listener's imagination. Do, therefore, be involved from start to finish; it is important.

A good radio advertisement can be especially difficult to create. Basically, you are wholly reliant on your script to create a memorable mental picture. Initially you need to decide the message you wish to impart – perhaps a special offer, a sale or a range of new goods – and any other important information which you must try to put across. Obviously, the listener needs to know who and where your business is and, where applicable, how long the sale or special offer lasts. Next you must decide which approach to adopt. Should the tone be humorous, nostalgic or dramatic? Do, however, remember that the advertisement will only last for a short time, possibly only 20 seconds, and you have little time to create a mood, set a scene or develop a story. Therefore, keep it simple, direct and brief.

In radio advertisements the speaker will often address the listener directly, firing the key points out against appropriate background music or noise. It is vitally important that you ensure the voice used is right for both the style of advertisement and the product or service being offered. Some business owners like to hear their own voice on radio, however inappropriate it may be. By all means record the advertisement yourself but only if your voice is suitable. For instance, a female voice may be inappropriate if you operate a builders' merchants, whilst a gruff male voice may not be appealing when the advertisement is for women's products. The voice should generally be warm, friendly, reassuring, yet authoritative. Listen to existing radio advertisements and various programme presenters, which will help you to get a feel for the right type of voice for your particular product or service. The radio station's production department will be able to offer a range of voices to choose from, so do be selective. Background music or noises are also important. Again, the radio station should have a full range of tapes available, enabling you to choose one which will enhance and develop the mood and theme of the advertisement.

Another very popular method used in radio advertisements is to create a dialogue between two characters, imparting the sales message as part of their conversation. This format certainly gives you more scope to use your imagination. Unfortunately, it can also increase the chances of producing a poor advertisement. We have all listened to this style of advertisement, where the advertiser is straining unsuccessfully to be humorous and ends up merely obscuring and detracting from his message. Any dialogue must be natural and well timed. It should sound like a real conversation rather than two actors simply reading their lines. There should be a reason for the conversation and the listener should feel he is overhearing two friends chatting. In order to achieve this, use simple, everyday words and phrases. Think about the characters. Give them life and substance, make them real people.

The next step is to personally record the draft advertisement on tape. This will help you judge its length and take the opportunity to cut out unnecessary words and phrases. Play the tape to colleagues and watch them carefully as they listen. If they do not laugh when they are supposed to or their attention wanders, then you may need to re-think the whole idea. If it cannot hold the attention of your colleagues, then it has little or no chance of succeeding with total strangers.

The draft tape should then be taken to the radio station who will offer any necessary advice. For example, they might suggest that the message would be improved if it were delivered more slowly, that it is better that the name of your company is mentioned at the start and finish rather than just at the end. They may advise you to drop the telephone number as few listeners will be able to write it down in time, and use that extra few moments to repeat details of the special offer instead. After these discussions they will professionally produce a draft copy. Check it through carefully and be critical. Is it really funny? Does it work in the way you envisaged? Do not be afraid, even at this stage, to amend the tape. It must be as near to perfect as possible. Do not settle for second best. You have a first class product or service to sell and it deserves a first class advertisement.

Creating a Good Poster

Posters are rarely used as the sole advertising medium. They are usually designed to remind potential customers of a product or service which is well established and advertised in another media format. As reminders, posters should be seen frequently, so try to choose the best possible site. Ideally, they should have a good, clear photograph or illustration with a big, bold headline across the top for maximum impact. Text across the bottom is more likely to be obscured by buses, cars and trees and so lose impact. Keep the entire poster simple, quick and easy to read and understand. The line 'Ah, Bisto' with a picture of the Bisto Kids is the perfect example of a poster which fulfils these basic principles. Take care not to be too clever or obscure – the average passerby may miss the point you are trying to make. A humorous approach can often be successful but do remember that tastes vary. Do, therefore, avoid anything which could be considered tasteless, vulgar or childish. Such an advertisement will simply alienate or offend those very people you wish to attract.

Posters, as previously discussed, can also be used to inform. However, they are more suited to areas where there is a 'captive' audience and where they can be used to explain a new product or detail a new business. When used for this purpose, the poster should follow the same basic rules as those for creating sales literature. In other words, they should be direct, to the point and brief in order to succeed.

The production of posters is a specialised job and you may need the assistance of an expert in producing yours. Individual poster contractors will always advise and The Outdoor Advertising Association will also offer helpful suggestions. (See page 39 for their address and telephone number.)

Creating Good Direct Mail

The creation of good direct mail takes skill and expertise. Advice can be obtained from organisations such as the Direct Mail Services Standards Board and The Direct Mail Producers Association. You may also decide to seek assistance from an experienced copy writer used to producing sales letters who would avoid many of the basic errors found in direct mail, which tend to irritate and annoy the recipient.

However, if you do intend to create your own letters then look carefully at the 'wrapper' in which you will send it. The envelope will be your first point of contact with the consumer and those which are clearly seen as being mailshots may be thrown unopened into the waste paper basket. Try, therefore, to arouse the recipient's curiosity and make him eager to open it. Your envelope should look smart, well presented and in line with corporate image. The recipient's name and address should be neatly and correctly typed with labels and stamps carefully placed. These may appear to be minor points but they all help to create the right impression. The recipient could be reluctant to buy from a company who mails cheap, incorrectly addressed envelopes, assuming their products are equally shoddy.

Obviously, the appearance of the envelope's contents are even more important. Again, sales letters should be well laid out, neatly and correctly typed on good quality paper. The text should be surrounded by clear margins, paragraphs be short and concise and the overall appearance co-ordinated and aesthetically pleasing. If the mailing is small and your personnel resources allow for it, it is a nice touch for each letter to be individually typed, carefully checked and signed. However, where the mailing is larger you will need to make use of a word processor or even approach a specialist company to carry out the project for you. Never try to photocopy sales letters and 'match up' individual names, addresses and salutations. The quality of reproduction will invariably be far from perfect and the end product will look cheap.

The contents of your letter need careful consideration and,

although they will vary depending upon the nature of the company, its products and services and the recipient to whom it is addressed, there are a number of common points to bear in mind. A good sales letter should never start with the general greeting such as 'Dear Sir, Madam or Customer'. Direct mail is a personal medium targeted at specific individuals. In fact that is one of its particular strengths. You know the potential customer's name and should use it. However, do not be too friendly or over-familiar. Many people will be irritated by the initial use of their christian name, especially by someone who is a stranger. Such presumption conjures up a mental image of the stereotype hard-sell salesman who, on being introduced for the first time, acts as though you have been lifelong friends. The tone of your letter may be friendly and informal but the greeting should be respectful – 'Dear Mr Sanderson'.

Where possible, keep your letter brief. If necessary, detailed information can be contained in an enclosed catalogue or leaflet. Use terms appropriate to the target audience. There is little point in using technical jargon when selling to the general public. They will probably be unable to understand it and this will make them feel stupid or assume that you are being patronising. If, however, you are addressing a technical expert the situation is reversed and they may feel offended if your message is too simplistic. Be friendly and pleasant but keep the tone and content of your letter pitched at the right level for the market at which it is aimed. Choose your words carefully and avoid over-long, convoluted sentences where the reader may lose track of your message.

Ideally, a sales letter should be around four or five paragraphs in length. The first paragraph is very important. In a way, it is the 'headline' in that it must attract attention and maintain interest. Develop your points and basic theme through the next two or three paragraphs, repeating the key message to remind the reader. Your final paragraph should urge the reader to act, and act now! For example, he may derive an extra benefit, say, 10 per cent discount, by replying immediately. Your main aim is to make him take a buying decision whilst your message is still strong in his mind.

Repetition is the key to advertising success and you may need to fire several shots to succeed. A campaign should last for a relatively short period of time but could, perhaps, consist of three mailshots. These should be sent at short intervals so that the previous message is still relatively fresh in the reader's memory but be cautious for too many letters on the same subject will irritate and finally infuriate. Selective multiple mailshots also give you the opportunity to vary the format and see which sales slant elicits the greatest response.

As already stressed, it is most important that the mailing list is totally accurate, and if you are using your own list, you must ensure it is kept up to date. The use of an outdated list is a waste of time and money. When buying in a list make sure to ask when the list was last used. Whilst you may be able to claim a refund from the list brokers on a list which is grossly out of date, you will still have wasted a considerable amount of effort and time to very little effect. Check also the type of people included on any list you buy in. Are they ABs, C2s or DEs? Do they fit the profile of your target market?

Creating a Good Exhibition Stand

When you choose to display your products at an exhibition, you firstly need to give careful consideration as to the choice of that exhibition. The press advertisement for a garden centre on the women's fashion pages of a magazine would be totally out of place. Similarly, a business selling specialised goods at a general consumer show may achieve little success. Choosing the right show is, therefore, of vital importance. The costs involved in exhibiting should lead to hard financial benefits, unless you specifically decide to use it merely as a showcase.

Consider the position of the stand. In a small show this may not be so important because visitors will circulate several times. At a larger show try to find a site near a large company who will attract a good flow of traffic, or close to the entrance or restaurant.

Unless you have a large budget to work with, choose a stand

which simply requires you to 'dress' it and exhibit your goods. This will avoid the extra cost of employing contractors or designers, although you might derive some benefit from contacting the British Exhibition Contractors Association whose address and telephone number can be found on page 36. If you are a first time exhibitor they will be happy to advise you.

Many exhibitors buy portable display units which can be purchased at reasonable prices from shopfitters or specialist outlets, who advertise regularly in *Yellow Pages* or *Exchange & Mart*. These units can be adapted for different shows and used to display exhibits, photographs, sales literature. They are easy to assemble, extend, collapse and store and, between shows, can be used in showrooms or as portable exhibitions. However, you would be well advised to hire such items from the contractors the first time, until you can assess the benefits of exhibiting and decide whether it is likely to be a regular feature of your overall marketing strategy.

The stand itself should be well co-ordinated and eye catching. Advertising material – posters, showcards, banners – need to be bold and attract attention. They should promote the company's corporate image and highlight selected items. For instance, you may have a new product being unveiled for the first time. Slogans and typefaces should comply with your company's house style. This will help to reinforce customer perception, will be familiar to them and, ultimately, make them feel more comfortable about approaching your stand.

Once you have attracted the customer to your stand, 'courtesy' is the byword. The stand may be beautifully co-ordinated, look attractive and have a full range of products on display, but if the visitor has to spend an interminable length of time waiting in a queue to speak to a salesman he will not take those facts into consideration. So, if there is sufficient space, ensure that there is someone available to greet visitors, and offer them a seat where they can sit and read through the company's literature while waiting to talk business. To some of you this may appear to be a waste of space where products could have been displayed but in an exhibition, where many stands offer similar products, it could just give you the edge.

Ensure also that there is a plentiful supply of literature available for distribution and a member of staff primed to demonstrate any working models you may have on the stand. The use of a video presentation will not only attract visitors, but will also help to maintain the interest of those waiting to speak with sales staff. See your stand not only as a showcase for your product but also as a business office and, once you have attracted the visitor onto it, do everything you can to keep him there until 'the business' has been conducted.

Finally, one of the main strengths of an exhibition is the face-to-face contact, so remember that you and your staff are also advertisements for your company. A clean, tidy person who is friendly, helpful and attentive will win orders. Those who are badly groomed, appear disinterested or talk down to visitors will not. Pay attention to your own appearance and that of your staff, it could be an important factor in influencing a potential customer to buy from your company rather than from another one.

The Daily Telegraph Business Enterprise Book, *How To Make Exhibitions Work for Your Business,* covers in detail all those areas which need to be taken into account to ensure successful, profitable exhibiting.

Creating Good Point of Sale Material

The key role of point of sale material is to remind the customer of a product or service at the precise moment when they are in a position to actually buy. It should provide the final nudge into action as they are passing by the shop window, wandering around the store or even standing, money in hand, at the cash register. An ideal example of good point of sale material is the Access sticker on the cash till. It will catch the customer's eye and might remind her that she needs to reserve her cash for some other outgoing and that she can achieve that objective by paying for her present purchase with her Access credit card.

When planning to produce point of sale material you need to

consider it from two angles. First, it must impart a sales message to the customer. As with posters, this message needs to be easy to see and understand. It is a back up medium and should echo the style, ideas and colours of the main campaign. The Barclaycard 'Open/Closed' sign on the shop door is essentially a replica of the customer's own Barclaycard in shape, design and colour. It is in a standard style which runs through all the company's advertising and the customer will notice it and, consciously or sub-consciously, will absorb the message. Copy should be brief and simple, photographs and illustrations attractive, eye catching and relevant. The material must stand out and demand attention. It need not be subtle, but it must be seen.

Second, your point of sale material has to appeal not only to the customer but also to the retailer. A large poster, stand or dumpbin might attract customers, but may be of very little interest or use to the retailer with minimal space available to house it. The most beautifully designed stand may simply not fit in. Posters and stickers may be the wrong colour. For example, a carefully colour co-ordinated fashion boutique might decide not to use a poster because it did not fit in with their overall colour scheme. Alternatively, its lifespan may be too short. Seasonally produced items, such as a Father Christmas display stand, may require too much effort to load and unload in the space of a few short weeks. Even trivial things can lead to unused point of sale material. The retailer could be reluctant to put posters up onto his wall because of the damage caused by drawing pins or sticky tape, stickers can be difficult to unpeel from their backing, stands sent without assembly instructions take up too much valuable time to put together, and so on. Point of sale material can only succeed and be cost effective if it is seen. It can only be seen if it is used. Therefore, it must also suit the retailer's requirements.

Ideally you should consult with your stockists, either directly or through your sales force, to see what they can use. Some may be willing to erect elaborate stands, but this proportion is likely to be relatively small. They are likely to be more willing to consider items such as calendars, clocks and door signs, which are of use to them as well as putting over your sales message. Talk to them and take their suggestions into account. It is better to leave your advertising money in the bank than spend it on material which will go straight into the retailer's dustbin.

Creating Good Sales Literature

Sales literature, such as leaflets, booklets and catalogues, will provide you with far more space for detailed information than any other medium. It is, however, still important that you keep to the standard advertising principles of simplicity, discipline and conciseness.

Start by summarising the proposed contents of your leaflet, brochure or catalogue. Plan out your text based on a list of buying points which will appeal to the reader. Then carefully re-read the text, cutting out superfluous words and sentences without detracting from your message. Next, plan out any photographs or illustrations you wish to use. These must be relevant and should be placed in close proximity to the text to which they relate. Nothing is more annoying for a reader than to have to search a page to link up text with a badly placed photograph.

At this stage approach a number of printers to obtain quotations for your sales literature. The majority of printers will offer advice on the most appropriate size, number of pages and type of materials to be used. Some will even show you how to cut costs, perhaps by folding pages in a different way to avoid wasteful blank sections or using illustrations rather than full colour photographs. Just as with any other supplier, shop around bearing in mind not only price but also print quality and ability to meet your deadline dates.

Statutory and Voluntary Controls

There are many statutes, such as the Trade Descriptions Acts of 1968 and 1972, and many voluntary codes, such as the British

Code of Advertising Practice, which are concerned with advertising. They exist to protect the consumer and ensure that advertisements are legal, decent, honest and truthful. The media through which you choose to launch any campaign will check the advertisements to ensure that they meet these basic requirements. Clearly there are cases – such as the use of 'knocking' copy – where it can be difficult for the media to judge if an advertisement contravenes these rules. For your own benefit you should ensure that your material stays within the rules laid down. Exaggeration, half truths and unfounded attacks on competition will only rebound on you, for such tactics rarely succeed in the longterm.

Details of voluntary codes of practice are available from The Advertising Standards Authority whose address and telephone number can be found on page 35. You can obtain details of statutory controls from your local Citizens Advice Bureau. Their address and telephone number will be in the telephone directory and they can supply a full range of leaflets on the relevant Acts.

9
The Media Schedule

Drafting Your Media Schedule

Before approaching the selected media you must draft a preliminary media schedule which will detail where, how and when you will advertise. Working within your advertising budget you will need to select individual organisations within the chosen media, decide on the correct type and style of advertisement and plan out the duration of the campaign and the frequency of advertising within that period. This jigsaw of different elements has to fit together, within the allocated budget, if you are to reach the target market and achieve the objectives you have set. It is a difficult and demanding task.

Choosing the individual media

By the time you come to prepare your schedule you will already have decided which media to use. You must then decide on specific radio stations, newspapers and magazines etc and how much of the budget is to be allocated to each. Clearly your aim is to obtain maximum penetration into your target market at the lowest possible cost. As previously indicated, research will highlight which publications, for example, are heavily read and more importantly, read by the right people. Similarly, researching rate cards, prices and circulations will indicate which are likely to prove cost effective.

Selecting the advertisement

You will already have decided on the style and layout of the advertisement to be used and will need to enter onto your schedule precisely when they will appear. In the case of press advertising, the location of the advertisement within a particular newspaper or journal should also be noted. Quite often the size of your advertising budget will have a strong influence on these decisions. For example, most journals charge extra for a solus advertising slot, which may make them less appealing to companies working on a smaller budget.

Choosing the frequency and duration of the campaign

Next you have to calculate how often your advertisements should be seen or heard and on which days, in which weeks, months and even seasons. This decision is invariably linked with the duration of your planned campaign. Also you need to decide whether to adopt a slow, steady approach to advertising over a longer period of time or to advertise in short, sharp bursts at specific times. Clearly, this can be a difficult decision. The manufacturer of a well established product may choose a small but regular campaign, while the producer of a new, innovative product may feel, in the early stages, that a short, intensive campaign using a variety of media and advertisements to bring his message home forcefully would be more beneficial.

For example, there are certain times of the year when customers are in either a 'buying' or 'saving' mood which would affect a campaign. In general there is little money to spare in, say, February when the public is counting the cost of Christmas and the January sales. A retailer advertising across that month would probably see very poor results from monies he had spent.

It is also difficult to decide just how often an advertisement should be seen or heard. At what point does the frequency of advertising achieve maximum impact? Not an easy question to answer. You will need to use your knowledge of the market to assess how often your advertisement needs to be seen to achieve the desired effect, and even then you may still get it wrong. Three or four times may be just right – maximum success for minimum expenditure. Below that number will possibly mean a wasted campaign and five or six may be wasteful too. Only experience and careful analysis of the results of previous campaigns will help you to get this judgement correct.

There is no such thing as the 'perfect' media schedule. No advertiser will ever know if he could have achieved greater success with less expenditure. All you can do is carefully assess the imponderables and, hopefully, outline a flexible plan where all the variables gel together. This is rarely achieved at the first attempt and so you must be prepared to change direction, if necessary.

Pre-testing

Every advertising campaign has an element of risk attached to it. Success can never be guaranteed. You can, however, minimise your chances of failure by exercising caution in planning your media schedule and carefully evaluating your campaign at every stage. Initially, the manufacturer of any successful product would have carefully researched his market to ascertain that there was a demand for his product. In addition, he would have judged its name, price, packaging and image to ensure maximum market appeal. Such a slow, step-by-step approach would allow him to highlight potential flaws in the overall project which, if not dealt with at this early stage, could prove costly. Similarly, the advertiser must test his campaign and monitor its development.

For example, it is sound practice to test your copy. Try to get feedback from colleagues and family and, if appropriate, organise a survey of members of the public. In the case of colleagues and members of the family, study their reactions, seek their views and absorb and act on constructive criticism. Your public survey should seek to ascertain how much information has been absorbed and retained and, most importantly, whether or not your key message has come across. Where your advertising is aimed at trade customers, the same principles still apply.

It is also a good idea to test the media before committing your company to a costly, long term campaign. If you decide to advertise in the press, for instance, book two or three insertions initially and monitor reaction to them before proceeding with your long term plans.

The Organisation of a Medium

During the early stages of your planning you will have researched the benefits and drawbacks of the various media available. It will also be helpful to have some knowledge of how a medium is organised before starting your campaign. In many ways, the chosen medium will act as a surrogate advertising agency offering advice, assistance and, in some cases, a comprehensive production service. There are a number of departments common to most media. Some will be amalgamated and, in the case of smaller organisations, may even be run by a single individual. Briefly, these departments are:

The editorial department

This department will usually dictate the style and content of the particular medium and, ideally, will endeavour to suit the mood, views and feelings of its audience, who may also form part of your target market. The good advertiser will regularly study editorial matter in, say, newspapers and magazines to ensure his advertisements compliment the overall tone and style. For example, a consumer advertisement designed for insertion in *The Daily Mirror* would be unlikely to be suitable for *The Times*.

The advertisement department

The prime objective of this department is to sell space, or air time, to advertisers. In many media it strikes a careful balance with the editorial department. The press, for example, usually survives on the basis of revenue from straight sales and income from advertising. It is a sound practice to build up a good working relationship with the advertisement manager or the representative who regularly handles your business. They will have a thorough knowledge of their medium and will be happy to indicate which locations, sizes and styles are best, thus helping you to formulate a more effective media schedule. They will also have an intimate knowledge of editorial policy and future plans, particularly in the case of the advertisement manager. Perhaps, for instance, special supplements are scheduled on specific subjects, one of which could be applicable to your business. In addition, they will also have access to information on the medium's audience, rival media and your competition, all of which you will find very useful.

The circulation/subscription department

These departments are mainly applicable to the press medium, although radio and television companies may have a department dealing with audience statistics. The role of the circulation department is to organise the physical distribution of the media and to ensure that the goods, such as newspapers and magazines, arrive at the right place at the right time. The subscription department deals with readers who subscribe to a magazine or newspaper on an annual or half-yearly basis. These subscribers will often form the basis of that particular medium's audience research. You should make use of this ready made research source and, of course, potential direct mail list.

The publicity department

Also termed the sales promotion or advertising department, its role is to promote the medium in order to increase circulation or build listening and viewing figures. Campaigns may operate on different levels and be aimed at the public who watch, listen to or read the medium, its potential advertisers who buy space or air time and, in the case of the press, the wholesalers and retailers who stock it. If possible, make contact with this department and make use of the information and experience of those who run it have built up.

The production department

This department is concerned with actually producing the media. Newspapers and magazines must be printed, poster sites constructed and maintained and television and radio program-mes broadcast. Unless you decide to 'do it yourself' or find alternative assistance, you will undoubtedly have dealings with this department. As already discussed, most media offer a full production service and if you decide to avail yourself of this facility a good working relationship with the appropriate members of this department will make the job much easier.

Of course, each medium is different. The publicity depart-ment may be termed the marketing or merchandising depart-ment, or may not exist at all. It may, for example, be run by a head office or separate organisation. Similarly, a research department may be incorporated within some media or, again, dealt with centrally.

As with all other facets of running a successful company, good contacts are very important. It is usually much easier to obtain information and advice from someone who knows you and your business than it is when speaking to someone who is a total stranger.

10

The Execution of a Campaign

Executing a Press Campaign

You may, of course, know from the start which newspapers and magazines you intend to use. If you do not, the latest copy of BRAD (address and telephone number can be found on page 36) will detail the majority of press available in the UK, divided into consumer and business categories. BRAD will also supply information on their individual rates, circulation figures, technical data and so on. With this information to hand you can then telephone or write to the advertisement manager to obtain a specimen copy of his publication and other relevant information which will help you make your final choice. If you prefer it, you can also arrange for an agent or representative to call and see you.

Rate card

Newspapers and magazines are likely to play a significant role in most campaigns and, as such, it is important that you have a good knowledge and understanding of the rate card and its terms, before booking space.

A rate card will include the name, address and telephone number of the advertisement department and may give a contact name. It will also state:

1. Frequency of publication – daily, evening, weekly or monthly.
2. Copy date – the deadline date for receipt of advertising copy or camera-ready artwork.
3. Cancellation terms – the length of notice required to cancel a

firm booking for advertising space and any penalties attached.
4. Actual publication dates.
5. Current circulation figures – usually ABC verified.
6. Technical details concerning the printing process.
7. Rates for varying sizes and types of advertisement.

There will also be a number of publishing terms used on the rate card with which you should familiarise yourself.

Run of paper is a term used for an advertisement, charged at a basic rate and located within the newspaper or magazine at their discretion.

Special position indicates that the advertisement will be placed in a specific location nominated by the advertiser and for which a higher rate has been paid.

Solus position means an advertisement which will be the only one on a particular page, again charged for at a higher rate.

Island position means that the advertisement will appear surrounded by editorial text.

Next matter indicates the advertisement will be placed next to editorial text.

Facing matter means it will be placed on a page which faces a page of complete editorial matter.

Bled off refers to an advertisement which is taken to the edge of a page for effect and is mainly applicable to magazines.

Ear or *Title corner* is the space to either side of the front page title.

Single column centimetre (SCC) is the nominal unit of advertising space sold by newspapers and magazines. It relates to the depth of an advertisement and the width is measured by the number of printed columns utilised. Cost can be calculated by multiplying the depth of the advertisement in centimetres by the width (number of columns) by the SCC rate. For example, an advertisement 10 cms long by three columns wide at a rate of £2.00 per SCC would cost £60 plus VAT.

Advertising space can also be bought in eighth, quarter, half or full pages and the rate for each of these will also appear on the rate card.

Line advertisement or *small advertisement* where the text is simply run across a single or multiple printed column.

Display advertisement is one where the text is laid out for maximum effect often using illustrations and a mixture of different type faces and sizes and usually surrounded by a border.

Classified advertisement is one placed under a classified heading, eg 'For Sale' or 'Wanted', and usually in line advertisement format.

Semi display refers to an advertisement in the classified section which is set out in a display fashion.

Spot colour indicates that a second colour, such as red or blue, can be used to highlight a particular feature, possibly a company name or logo.

It will also be useful for you to know something about the method used to actually print the newspaper or magazine. Three main processes are used and they are known as letterpress, lithography and photogravure.

Letterpress is a technique whereby a raised, inked surface comes into contact with the paper in order to produce printed copy. This method of printing means that a newspaper, for example, can be quickly and easily produced.

Lithography means that the printed image is produced on a metal plate which is treated with a greasy substance receptive to ink. The plate is then dampened with water and when spread with ink the greased printed image, which has repelled the water, takes up the ink. The inked plate prints onto a rubber blanket which in turn prints onto paper. This 'offset' printing method means that the plate will last longer because it is more resilient to wear and tear.

Photogravure indicates that the printed image has been etched onto a printing plate. This process is relatively slow and expensive and is usually used on magazines where the large print run makes it economically viable.

If the product or service you wish to advertise is particularly newsworthy, or the newspaper or magazine is running a special edition to which it is particularly relevant, you may also be able to arrange for editorial coverage. Just like any other manufacturer, newspapers and magazines need to sell their product and in order to do so must fill their pages with matter their customers want to read. So never be reluctant to approach them if you feel there is something of particular interest about your company or its products or services. Your story could be just what they are looking for. Remember also that favourable editorial comment about your company will be perceived by the reader as an unbiased and independent endorsement – a very persuasive factor in their final decision on whether or not to buy.

Executing a Radio Campaign

Most advertisers planning a radio campaign will normally approach their local independent radio station direct. Addresses and telephone numbers will be listed in *Yellow Pages*. Alternatively, if you wish to advertise on a number of stations you could contact one of the two national sales offices selling air time across the regions. They are:

Southern Region
Independent Radio Sales Ltd (IRS)
86–88 Edgware Road
London W2 2EA
01–258 0408

Northern Region
Broadcast Marketing Services (BMS)
7 Duke of York Street
St James's Square
London SW17 6LA
01–839 4151

A radio rate card will be sent to you on request, indicating the cost of basic spots at different times of the day and week. These will vary in price according to the listening figures at the time. For example, advertising in the peak listening period between 6.00 am and 9.00 am will be more costly than advertising in the evening when listening figures are lower. However, it could be that when you study the breakdown of audience figures for the station, you will find that early evening advertising will penetrate further into your target marketplace than morning advertising. Radio advertising is normally sold in transmissions of 10, 20, 30, 40, 50 and 60 second blocks and, on commercial radio, is available for around 9 minutes in every hour. Most radio stations offer a variety of packages, for example, a 'daytime package' where a number of advertisements are guaranteed transmission between 6.00 am and 6.00 pm. Alternatively, and likely to be more expensive than a general discount package, advertising can be arranged for particular programmes or even around weather forecasts, traffic reports or the 8.00 am news peak.

Study the rate card and other information supplied before deciding what you want. Then spend some time listening to the radio during the proposed advertising period to get a feel for the programmes and other advertisements being broadcast at that time. Note the style and content of these other advertisements to see which are particularly memorable. Once you are satisfied with the outcome of your research, contact the station or ask for a sales representative to call and see you. Then proceed to negotiate the best possible deal. Rate cards can be varied and a new advertiser, promising substantial future business, may be offered certain extra discounts or benefits.

Discuss the ideas you have for your specific advertisement; the station's staff will be able to offer practical advice and help.

As already discussed, you would be well advised initially to use the production facilities of the station in creating your advertisement. Armed with your preliminary ideas and samples of your sales literature to aid creation, they will then prepare a draft tape for your comment and approval. Listen carefully to the tape and try to assess whether it would stand out in a crowd. At this stage you still have the option of amending, or even scrapping the advertisement if you feel it is completely wrong.

Once your campaign is underway, monitor it carefully to

ensure that the advertisements are being transmitted at the right times. Do not be afraid to be critical and let the radio station know if you are dissatisfied in any way.

Executing a Poster Campaign

BRAD will also provide you with details of outdoor poster sites available from a range of organisations. These include poster contractors such as Mills and Allen, More O'Ferrall, London and Provincial and Arthur Maiden; transport companies such as London Transport Advertising and British Transport Advertising; and local authorities. It supplies specific information on poster advertising on static sites, ranging from hoardings, through bus shelters to litter bins and parking meters. Under the heading 'Transport', you will find details of advertising opportunities in taxis, on tube trains, ships and even air advertising.

Having made your selection of potential sites, you will then need to contact the organisations who own or administer them. If you have had your eyes on, say, a particular billboard near your business, you can check it out to ascertain the owners and approach them direct for details of terms and costs. You can advertise on one particular site, or buy a package of sites based in an area and can advertise for periods from one month to an indefinite term contracted on a 'till countermanded' basis. Costs obviously vary according to length of campaign, position of sites and size of posters.

Once sites have been booked and your posters are in place, make sure they are inspected regularly. This not only enables you to ensure that the posters remain in good condition but will also allow you to re-assess a site's ongoing suitability for your advertising needs.

Executing a Cinema Campaign

For many smaller companies the cost of producing acceptable

advertising film for the cinema, and indeed for television, is too prohibitive. However, your local cinema should be able to offer a choice of pre-made stock films, which allow around 15 seconds at the end for your name, address and telephone number to either appear on the screen or be 'voiced over'.

Initially you will need to spend some time in the cinema to gauge the make-up of a typical audience, get a 'feel' for the atmosphere and, most importantly, satisfy yourself about the quality of the stock films on offer. In many cases these may be of indeterminate age and could be totally inappropriate for your particular image.

If you do decide to proceed, the cinema – depending on who its owners are – will put you in touch with the sales contractor who handles their advertising. Generally this will be either Pearl and Dean or Rank and they will supply details of the packages available. Your advertisement can be shown for as little as one week on one screen, although 10 to 12 weeks is considered the optimum time to mount an acceptable and successful campaign. The advertisement will be shown once at every performance, just before the main feature. Experience has shown that after 20 to 26 weeks the sales effect tends to level off as the repetition factor grows. Therefore, if you decide to use this medium on an ongoing basis, you will ideally need to produce at least two, and probably even three, different advertisements to cover one year's campaign. Even using stock films, which would need to be carefully selected to ensure they are of good quality and complement your company's image, this would be an expensive exercise. Bearing in mind the comments already made in Chapter 4, this is a medium for use selectively and then only after careful research.

Executing a Direct Mail Campaign

Having carried out your initial research, you will already have decided whether to use the services of a direct mail organisation or whether to undertake the exercise within your own company.

If you have decided to use an outside contractor, there will still need to be continuous liaison to ensure that your instructions are carried out fully. As far as the recipient is concerned the mailing has come from you and if it is sub-standard in any way, this will reflect badly on your company and not the direct mail house. You may never use their services again, but the damage which has been done within your target market will be difficult to repair.

The chances are, however, that you will have to undertake the project within your own company, using all available resources.

Quite apart from acquiring mailing lists and producing sales literature, you will need to take into account the physical constraints of implementing such a mailing. You will need to allow for the time it actually takes to produce a personalised letter, even using word processors and high speed printers, and a properly addressed envelope. The contents of the envelope will have to be collated, folded and inserted. The envelopes then have to be sealed, stamped or franked and, unless your mail is collected, taken to the post office. Do not forget, also, that since the whole concept of direct mail is based around the idea that the potential customer receives a personalised letter, either you or your sales manager will probably have to sign each one individually. Depending on the total size of the mailer, this could prove to be a very time consuming exercise.

Unless you have access to sophisticated mailing equipment which will collate, fold, insert, then seal and frank the envelopes automatically, the whole exercise is very labour intensive. Consider whether you have sufficient staff to handle it without detriment to their normal jobs, or whether you will need to take on some additional labour to help out.

Once the mailing has been despatched and replies start to come back, they will need to be logged and analysed for future use. For example, any envelopes which are returned marked 'Gone Away' can be used to delete those names and addresses as part of your list cleaning process. Keep a record of the additional sales generated by the mailing to show how effective, or otherwise, it has been as an advertising tool. The answer to this question could have a direct effect on your future advertising plans.

Advertising at an Exhibition

To obtain details of forthcoming exhibitions and their organisers, you can either consult BRAD once again or one of the monthly journals such as *Exhibitions and Conferences Gazette* or *Conferences and Exhibitions International*. Information can also be obtained from trade associations, trade magazines or your local chamber of commerce.

Once you have decided on the most appropriate exhibition to take part in, approach the organisers who will supply information on the proposed layout, available sites, rates, projected attendance figures and other general statistics. You may also know of other companies who have participated in this particular exhibition in past years. If you do, it will be worth your while to contact them for their opinion. They will speak from the exhibitor's point of view and from personal experience and you may get a slightly different picture and more practical advice than that to be gleaned from the organiser's literature and statistics.

With this information to hand, if you then decide to proceed, book the best site you can afford. Most stands comprise a basic unit with walls, carpeted base and standard lighting. A company name strip will also be supplied to fit across the front of the stand. Any additional stand furniture such as chairs, tables, shelving, display stands, can be hired through the organisers or supplied yourself. You will also be allocated a time during which you have access to the exhibition hall to set up your stand and, at the finish of the exhibition, dismantle it and remove your exhibits. If you wish to make any major changes or additions to the stand you should consult the organisers who will give you the name of an authorised contractor to undertake the work. Advice can also be obtained from:

British Exhibition Contractors Association
Kingsmere House
Wimbledon
London SW19 3SR
01–543 3888

You would also be advised to get in touch at an early stage with the exhibition's press officer to make sure that you take full advantage of all the publicity surrounding the event. In addition to your standard entry in the catalogue, you may also decide to insert an advertisement and this will need to be prepared in good time.

Anyone considering overseas exhibitions needs to consult not only the organisers but also the Department of Enterprise (regional office addresses will be found in your telephone directory) and:

British Overseas Trade Board (BOTB)
1 Victoria Street
London SW1H 0EY
01–215 7877

Your local chamber of commerce will also be able to offer advice and assistance.

Buying Miscellaneous Services

Should you decide not to use the services offered by the various media organisations, there are a number of specialists with whom you will need to get into contact to help you produce leaflets, catalogues, brochures and point of sale material. These will include:

Printers

Some printers specialise in particular areas of printing but there are many general printers whose addresses and telephone numbers can be found in your local *Yellow Pages* or business directory. Many of these printers will also offer a design facility and will be a source of help in choosing the right paper or material. They will also supply advice on page sizes, folds and other general printing information. Quotations for artwork, design, platemaking and printing can vary considerably so, as with any other supplier, shop around for the best deal.

Photographers

You may require photographs to be taken for use as illustrations in sales and advertising material. Again, telephone numbers and addresses of local commercial photographers can be found in local business directories. Do use a commercial photographer where possible, to obtain the most professional results. As with your printer, you should shop around for the best possible deal.

Artists/designers

Whilst many printers will offer a design facility you should bear in mind that, often, the results will owe more to draughts-manship than creativity. To employ a commercial artist specialising in your area may cost more initially but is likely to lead to more creative results. Supply the artist with your initial ideas and as much information about your product as possible. The more he has to work with, the better will be the finished article.

Once the campaign is underway, your involvement is far from over, as you then move on to the process of continuous evaluation.

11

Evaluating Results

It is important that you are prepared to spend time constantly reviewing your advertising campaign and checking the results in order that future advertising – and budgets – can be adjusted accordingly. You need to know if your objectives were achieved, whether the campaign was designed to launch a new product, increase sales or change the product's image. Also, was the form of advertising selected the right one? Did you choose the most suitable medium, the best position or timing and the correct size of advertisement? Did the campaign achieve maximum success for minimum expenditure or could a little extra advertising, perhaps in a different medium, have substantially increased sales? Conversely, could the same results have been achieved with a lower level of expenditure?

If an advertising campaign appears to have failed, perhaps because a sales target was not reached, try to analyse the reasons for this in order that future campaigns do not make the same mistakes. The campaign may have been poor creatively or the advertisements may not have been seen by enough people. On the other hand, it may have failed for any number of external reasons totally unconnected with advertising. It must be stressed that advertising forms only one part of the overall business strategy and should never be judged in isolation. The success or failure of a campaign can be affected not only by the actual advertisement, its position and the choice of media but also by other factors such as the product's price, quality, perceived image, distribution and competitive activity. As an individual entity advertising should be assessed and be accountable, but the advertiser must lookk at the *total* picture when making a judgement. For example, a campaign may have been launched in the early summer for a new range of ice creams with the objective of selling a set amount by a given date. However, a cold, wet summer with very few sunny days would probably mean that the target was not achieved, despite an excellent advertising campaign. On the other hand, the weather may be perfect but the ice cream too expensive, wrongly packaged or perhaps competition launched a similar range at the same time, more competitively priced and attractively packaged.

Even meticulous research and analysis is unlikely to provide the answer to every question. A campaign may fail for reasons which are overlooked or never identified. For instance, the original objectives could have been unrealistic, too generalised or, even, too specific. Even if it succeeds you will probably never know if it could have been better. Often you will be trying to measure the unmeasurable – but you must still try.

There are a number of ways of evaluating results, depending upon the objectives which were set. It is up to you to select the one most appropriate to your campaign. You may have set objectives to invite enquiries, to sell direct, to expand or to maintain the market, to obtain more stockists or to recruit staff. Such objectives are relatively easy to measure, simply by counting the number of replies received and noting how many are converted into new sales, new stockists and new members of staff. A manufacturer seeking 40 new stockists, who runs a short series of advertisements in a trade magazine and receives 200 replies which are eventually converted into 50 new stockists, would undoubtedly consider his campaign to have been successful.

However, evaluating a campaign is not always so easy. You may have advertised in two or three newspapers and found that over 90 per cent of enquiries used the coupon from just one of them. The question you then have to try and answer is, would the same results have been achieved using just that one newspaper?

Ideally, every advertisement should be coded with a reference number printed on the clip coupon, voucher, freepost or prepaid envelope. Alternatively, the customer may be invited to telephone a certain number or write to a certain person or department. For example, your radio advertisement could urge people to contact Mrs Reynolds whereas your press advertisement named Mrs Stephens. The level of response to each of them would allow you to ascertain precisely where and when the customer saw or heard the advertisement.

A direct response campaign is simple to assess in terms of replies, but also has other measurable benefits. It can, for example, help to gauge what elements of a product are considered most important. The same basic advertisement can be slightly varied, with each variation promoting a different feature (e.g. price, reliability, appearance) to see which is most appealing to the buying public. Similarly, by coding the different advertisements you can also judge which sizes, positions, colours, styles and days of the week bring the best response. This form of advertising can also highlight which media is most suitable, in which area and to which people. Clearly, the number of coupons returned can be compared for each individual newspaper and magazine used and can, if carefully analysed, indicate which geographic area they are from and whether they have been sent back by men or women.

Coupons can also be used to measure the number of replies and what percentage are eventually converted into sales. From this you will be able to measure whether or not the campaign has been cost effective or if, in future, the different elements involved need to be varied in any way. Finally, returned direct response coupons can also form the basis for building up your own mailing lists for future direct mail campaigns.

The success of certain campaigns can be measured without the need to use codings. A campaign aimed at stockists can measure its success by checking the salemen's order books. Similarly, an advertiser with the objective of launching a new product, can gauge the response to his advertising by counting how much product has moved off his shelves. If you are selling on a national basis and your budget allows for it, you might even choose to employ a company to measure results in retail outlets on a sales audit basis.

Clearly, it is not always possible to evaluate a campaign easily, especially if there is a 'generalised' objective of making an announcement, reminding customers or changing the product or company image. The campaign may well be measurable in terms of sales but this is likely to be a long term development. If you wish to measure the short term effect, you could choose to instigate a series of consumer surveys. These can be carried out by telephone, writing to consumers or simply stopping people in the street and asking them relevant questions, or you could gather a number of people together in one place and question them within a group environment. Such research can take place on an *ad hoc* basis. If, however, your objective had been to change the product's image, you would need to run two surveys, one before and one after the advertising campaign.

The assessment of an advertising campaign can bring many benefits. You may discover a whole new market for your products or services. It can help to eliminate the use of inappropriate media or indicate some adjustment which can help to save expenditure in the future. Whatever its effects, you will undoubtedly have gained in experience and expertise, which can only be of benefit in planning and implementing future advertising campaigns.

Bibliography

You may find the following books a useful source of information, advice and practical assistance.

Advertisers Annual (Kellys Directories).
Advertising Association Handbook (Advertising Association).
Advertising Layout Techniques, H Borgman (Watson Guptill).
All About PR, Roger Hayward (McGraw Hill).
Assessing the Effectiveness of Advertising, Jack Potter and Mark Lovell (Business Books).
Be Your Own PR Man, Michael Bland (Kogan Page).
Benns Press Directory (Benn Publications).
Creative Advertising, David Bernstein (Longman).
Design and Print Your Own Posters, J I Biegeleisen (Watson Guptill).
Direct Mail, Robin Fairlie (Kogan Page).
How to Advertise, Kenneth Roman and Jane Maas (Kogan Page).
How to Make Exhibitions Work for Your Business (Telegraph Publications).
Management Guide to Market Research, James Livingstone (MacMillan).
Marketing Pocket Book (The Advertising Association).
Market Research for Managers, Sunny Crouch (Heinemann).
Marketing Your Business, Jeremy Bond and Mike Tintner (Telegraph Publications).
Public Relations, Frank Jefkins (Macdonald and Evans).
The Art of Advertising, B Holme (Peerage Books).
The Complete Guide to Advertising, T Douglas (Macmillan).
The Dartnell Direct Mail and Mail Order Handbook, R S Hodgson (Dartnell).

The Secrets of Successful Copywriting, Patrick Quinn (Heinemann).
Twenty Four Ways to Improve your Direct Mail Results, J Kobs (Dartnell).

There are also a number of magazines and journals covering the subject of advertising and related areas. Details of these can be found in *British Rate and Data (BRAD)*.

Index

Telegraph
PUBLICATIONS

Telegraph Publications publishes a number of personal finance/business books as follows:

Britain on Business £8.95
Consumer's Guide to Buying and Selling a Home £5.95
Consumer's Guide to Student Finance £5.95
Cashflow and Credit Management £6.95
Club Treasurer's Handbook £10.95
Consumer's Guide to Lump-Sum Investment £5.95
Corporation Tax: A Working Guide for the Small Business £6.95
Daily Telegraph Expatriates' Tax and Investment Guide £6.95
Daily Telegraph Pensions Guide £10.95
Daily Telegraph Personal Tax Guide £5.95
Divorce and Separation £5.95
How to Choose Microcomputers & Software for Your Business £6.95
How to Choose the Right Business Premises £6.95
How to Export £6.95
How to Make Exhibitions Work for Your Business £6.95
How to Set Up and Run Conferences and Meetings £6.95
How to Set Up and Run Your Own Business £5.95
Lindsay Cook's Money Book £4.95
Making Your Business Efficient £6.95
Marketing Your Business £6.95
Mastering Business Information Technology £6.95
Money Matters for Students £1.95
Motivating Through Incentives £6.95
PAYE: A Working Guide for the Small Business £6.95
Personal Equity Plans £5.95
Planning For Retirement £5.95
Selecting and Managing Personnel £6.95
Stocks and Shares £5.95
Successful Borrowing and Coping with Debt £5.95
Tax: A Working Guide for the Self-Employed £6.95
The Marketing and Selling of Financial Services £14.95
Understanding Company Accounts £6.95
Unit Trusts £5.95
VAT: A Working Guide for the Small Business £6.95
With Government Approval £1.95
101 Ways of Investing and Saving Money £2.95
101 Ways of Saving Tax £1.95
101 Ways to run a Business Profitably £2.95

All these books are available through all good bookshops, or mail order from Telegraph Publications, PO Box 276, High Wycombe, Bucks HP12 4NN (adding 55p per book postage and packing).